The Blues Fakebook

Over 200 blues songs from the twenties to the present are included in this deluxe edition.
Many artists representing a wide variety of styles are featured; in addition, rare photographs are included.

by Woody Mann

Photographs by David Gahr

Oak Publications
New York • London • Paris • New York

Order No. OK 64983
US International Standard Book Number: 0.8256.1417.1
UK International Standard Book Number: 0.7119.3717.6

Exclusive Distributors:
Music Sales Corporation
257 Park Avenue South, New York, NY 10010 USA
Music Sales Limited
8/9 Frith Street, London W1V 5TZ England
Music Sales Pty. Limited
120 Rothschild Street, Rosebery, Sydney, NSW 2018, Australia

Printed in the United States of America by
Vicks Lithograph and Printing Corporation

Contents

Preface

The songs in this collection are culled from eighty years of blues performances representing many styles and composers. These songs illustrate the wide spectrum of sounds that make up an undefinable, yet recognizable music. The music and repertoire of blues artists is an inseparable and fundamental part of jazz, rock, folk, and pop music. It is these broad ranging influences that I tried to highlight in selecting the contents.

Since blues playing is basically improvisational, the lead sheets in this fakebook serve as a starting point for further individual variations. These transcriptions are straightforward, and they spell out the basic chords, melody, and the complete lyrics. Rather than write out the vocal interpretations of a particular performance, the song is laid out in its general (less confusing) form. The leadsheets are not written with any particular instrument in mind; therefore, the music is accessible to a greater number of musicians.

I would like to thank the many publishers that were cooperative and helpful. However, there were a quite a few companies that were unwilling to grant permissions for the songs and composers they represent. In many instances, they refused to license even one song (of many they control) so that a particular artist could be represented. The fact that many of the writers have passed away and left no estate, it seems, has empowered these companies to adopt a more self-serving agenda. Whatever their reasons are, it is ironic that some of the 'blues publishers' who represent the composers, are the very ones that are responsible for locking away the music. This type of attitude keeps many of the important and lesser known artists even farther out of public sight than they already are. There were many titles that I had to omit because of these legal entanglements; nevertheless, I am happy with the end result. This collection represents some of the greatest blue songs ever written.

I would like to thank Chris Owens for his help in gathering the recordings and Peter Pickow and Zoraya Mendez-De Cosmis at Music Sales for all their valuable assistance in putting this project together. And finally, special thanks to all the publishing houses who did understand a need for a collection like this.

Woody Mann
New York

Willie Dixon

Statesboro Blues

Recorded by: Blind Willie McTell

You're a mighty mean woman, to do me this a-way.(2X)
Going to leave this town, pretty mama, going away to stay.

I once loved a woman, better than I ever seen.(2X)
Treat me like I was a king and she was a doggone queen.

Sister, tell your Brother, Brother tell your Auntie, Auntie, tell your Uncle,
Uncle tell my Cousin, Cousin tell my friend.
Goin' up the country, Mama, don't you want to go?
May take me a fair brown, may take me one or two more.

Big Eighty left Savannah, Lord, and did not stop.
You ought to saw that colored fireman when he got that boiler hot.
Reach over in the corner, hand me my travelin' shoes.
You know by that, I got them Statesboro blues.

Sister got 'em, Daddy got 'em,
Brother got 'em, Mama got 'em,
Woke up this morning, we had them Statesboro blues.
I looked over in the corner,
Grandpa and Grandma had 'em too.

Rolling Log Blues

Recorded by: Lottie Kimbrough

Like a log, I've been jammed on the bank,
So hungry, I've grown lean and lank.

Get me a pick and shovel, dig down in the ground,
Gonna keep on digging till the blues come down.

I've got the blues for my sweet man in jail,
Now the judge won't let me go his bail.

I've been rolling and drifting from shore to shore,
Gonna fix it so I won't have to drift no more.

Good Morning Blues

New Words and New Music arranged by Huddie Ledbetter
Edited and New Additional Material by Alan Lomax

Recorded by: Leadbelly

Laid down last night, turnin' from side to side.(2X)
I was not sick, but I was just dissatisfied.

When I got up this mornin', blues walkin' round my bed.(2X)
I went to eat my breakfast, the blues was all in my bread.

I got a new way of spelling Memphis, Tennessee.(2X)
Double E, double T, Lord, double X-Y-Z

I sent for you yesterday, here you come walking today.(2X)
You got your mouth wide open, you don't know what to say.

Big Joe Williams

Make Me a Pallet on Your Floor
Ain't No Tellin'

by Mississippi John Hurt

Recorded by: Mississippi John Hurt

I'd be more than satisfied,
If I could reach that train and ride.
If I reach Atlanta with no place to go,
Make me a pallet on your floor.

Gonna give everybody my regards,
Even if I have to ride the rods.
If I reach Atlanta with no place to go,
Make me a pallet on your floor.

A Good Woman is Hard to Find

Recorded by: Champion Jack Dupree

Last ___ night, ___ I lost ___ the best friend, ___ yes, _____ in the world, _____ I ev - er did have. I say last night, oh ___ Lord, ___ best friend I had.

Lost a good woman and I grieve night and day.(2X)
Always keep worrying, since you went away.

Well nowadays a good woman is so hard to find.(2X)
When you think you got a good woman, yes, you got the other kind.

All I want is someone to love.(2X)
Lord I'm lonely, as I could be.

Nowadays a real good woman.(2X)
A real good woman, oh yeah, is hard to find.

One More Drink

by Elmore James

Recorded by: Elmore James

Give me one more drink, dar - ling, to cool my parch - ing

throat. _ Yes, give me one more drink, dar - ling,

to cool my parch-ing throat. _ I'm in love with you, ba - by,

and know I don't mean no wrong.

I'm in love with a woman, she treats me awful bad.(2X)
I spent a lot of money, now she don't pay me no mind.

Colonal Bill Williams

Trouble in Mind

Recorded by: Bertha "Chippie" Hill
Big Bill Broonzy
Brownie McGee/ Sonny Terry

Trou- ble in mind, I'm blue, _____ But I

won't be blue al - ways, 'Cause the sun's gon- na shine _____

_____ In my back door _____ some - day. _____

I'll gonna lay my head
On a lonesome railroad line,
And let the Two Nineteen pacify my mind.

I'm all alone at midnight,
And my lamp is turning low,
Never had so much trouble in my life before.

I'll gonna lay my head
On that lonesome railroad track,
But when I hear that whistle, Lord, I'm gonna pull it back.

You've been a hard-headed daddy,
And you sure treat me unkind,
I'll be a hard-headed mama, I swear I'll make you lose your mind.

I'm going down to the river,
Take along my rocking chair,
And if the blues don't leave me, I'll rock on away from here.

Look here, sweet mama,
See what you have done,
You made me love you, now your regular man done come.

Trouble in mind, I'm blue,
Trouble on my worried mind,
When you see me laughing, I'm laughing just to keep from crying.

John Henry

Recorded by: Leadbelly
Pete Seeger
Big Bill Broonzy

The captain said to John Henry,
"I'm gonna bring that steam drill around.
I'm gonna bring that steam drill out on the job,
I'm gonna whup that steel on down, Lord, Lord."(4X)

John Henry told his captain,
"Lord, a man ain't nothing but a man.
But before I'd let your steam drill beat me down,
I'd die with a hammer in my hand, Lord, Lord."(4X)

John Henry said to his shaker,
"Shaker, why don't you sing?
Because I'm swinging thirty pounds from my hips on down.
Just to listen to that cold steel ring, Lord, Lord."(4X)

Now the captain said to John Henry,
"I believe that mountain's caving in."
John Henry said right back to the captain,
"Ain't nothing but my hammer sucking wind, Lord, Lord."(4X)

Now the man that invented the steam drill,
He thought he was mighty fine.
But John Henry drove fifteen feet,
The steam drill only made nine, Lord, Lord.(4X)

John Henry hammered in the mountains,
His hammer was striking fire.
But he worked so hard, it broke his poor, poor heart,
And he laid down his hammer and he died, Lord,Lord.(4X)

See See Rider

Recorded by: Ma Rainey

I'm gonna buy me a pistol, just as long as I am tall, Lord, Lord, Lord.
Shoot my man, and catch a cannonball.
If he won't have me, he won't have no gal at all.

See See Rider, where did you stay last night? Lord, Lord, Lord.
Your shoes ain't buttoned and your clothes don't fit you right.
You didn't come home till the sun was shining bright.

Diddie Wa Diddie

Recorded by: Blind Blake

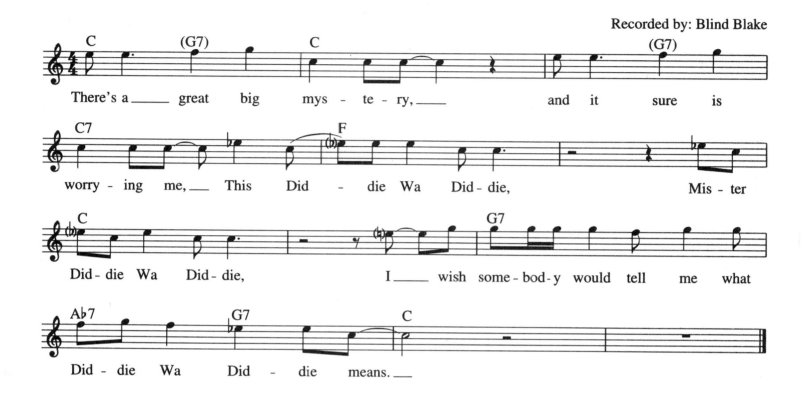

There's a ___ great big mys - te - ry, ___ and it sure is

worry - ing me, ___ This Did - die Wa Did - die, Mis - ter

Did - die Wa Did - die, I ___ wish some - bod-y would tell me what

Did - die Wa Did - die means. ___

The little girl about four feet four,
Come on papa and give me some more,
Of your Diddie Wa Diddie,
Your Diddie Wa Diddie,
I wish somebody would tell me what Diddie Wa Diddie means.

I went around and walked around,
Somebody yelled, said, "Look who's in town,"
Mister Diddie Wa Diddie,
Mister Diddie Wa Diddie,
I wish somebody would tell me what Diddie Wa Diddie means.

Went to church, put my hand on the seat,
Lady sat on it said, "Daddy, you sure is sweet,"
Mister Diddie Wa Diddie,
Mister Diddie Wa Diddie,
I wish somebody would tell me what Diddie Wa Diddie means.

I said,"Sister, I'll soon be gone,
Just gimme that thing you sitting on,"
Mister Diddie Wa Diddie,
Mister Diddie Wa Diddie,
I wish somebody would tell me what Diddie Wa Diddie means.

Then I got put out of church,
'Cause I talk about Diddie Wa Diddie too much,
Mister Diddie Wa Diddie,
Mister Diddie Wa Diddie,
I wish somebody would tell me what Diddie Wa Diddie means.

Sun's Going to Shine in My Back Door

Recorded by: Big Bill Broonzy
Sonny Terry/
Brownie McGee

Sit - tin' here hun - gry, _____ ain't got a dime, _ Looks like my friends would come to see me some - time. _____ But it won't mat - ter _____ how it hap - pens, The sun's gon- na shine in my door _ some - day. _____

When I was in jail, expecting a fine,
When I went before that judge, not a friend could I find.
But it won't matter how it happens,
The sun's gonna shine in my door someday.

I lost my father, I lost my brother too,
That's why you hear me singing, I'm lonesome and blue.
But it won't matter how it happens,
The sun's gonna shine in my door someday.

Lord, Lord, Lordy Lord,
I used to be your regular, now I got to be your dog.
But it won't matter how it happens,
The sun's gonna shine in my door someday.

I'm in trouble, no one to pay my fine,
When I get out this time, gonna leave this town flyin'.
But it won't matter how it happens,
The sun's gonna shine in my door someday.

I was with my buddy through thick and thin,
My buddy got away, and I got in.
But it won't matter how it happens,
The sun's gonna shine in my door someday.

Corrina, Corrina

Recorded by: Mississippi John Hurt
Josh White

Cor - rin - a, Cor - rin - a, where'd you stay last night?

Cor - rin - a, Cor - rin - a,

where'd you stay last night? Come

in this morn - ing, clothes ain't fit - tin' you right.

I left Corrina, way across the sea. (2X)
She wouldn't write me no letter, she don't care for me.

Oh Corrina, Corrina, where you been so long? (2X)
She wouldn't write me no letter, she don't care for me.

Corrina, Corrina, where you stay last night?(2X)
Come in this morning, clothes don't fit you right.

Mingelwood Blues

by Noah Lewis

Recorded by: Gus Cannon

Oh, I was born in the des - ert, I was raised in a
li - on's den. _____ Oh, I was
born in the des - ert, I was raised in the li - on's den. _____
And my reg - 'lar oc - cu - pa - tion is
tak - in' wom - en from _ their men. _

Don't you ever let no woman worry your mind.(2X)
'Cause she will keep you ragged and funny all the time.

Well, if you go by Memphis, please stop by Mingelwood.(2X)
'Cause the women in the camp don't mean no man no good.

Kokomo Blues

by Fred McDowell

Recorded by: Francis "Scrapper" Blackwell

Mmm,___ ba - by, don't you want___ to go.

Mmm, ba - by, don't you want to go.___

Pack your lit - tle suit - case,___

Pa - pa's goin' to Ko - ko - mo.

Mmm, baby, where you been so long?(2X)
I can tell, mama, something's going on wrong.

Mmm, baby, you don't know, you don't know.(2X)
Papa's all ready, going back to Kokomo.

And me and my baby had a falling out last night.(2X)
Somehow ain't nothing, and my babe won't treat me right.

Mmm, baby, what's the matter now?(2X)
Tryin' to quit your daddy, but you don't know how.

And I'll sing this verse, baby, I can't sing no more.(2X)
My train is ready, and I'm going to Kokomo.

Roll and Tumble

Recorded by: Hambone Willie Newbern

And I roll and I ____ tum-ble, and I cried the whole __ night long, ____

And I roll and I ____ tum-ble, and I cried the whole __ night long, __

And I rose this morn-ing, ma-ma, and I did-n't know __ right from wrong. __

Did you ever wake up and find your dough roller gone?(2X)
And you wring your head and you cry the whole night long.

And I told my woman just before I left the town.(2X)
Don't she let nobody tear her barrelhouse down.

And I fold my arms and I slowly walked away.(2X)
Say, that's alright, mama, your trouble gonna come someday.

Midnight Special

New words and new music adaptation by Huddie Ledbetter
Collected and Adapted by John A. Lomax and Alan Lomax

Recorded by: Leadbelly

verse

Well, you wake up in the morn - ing, ____ Hear the ding dong ring. ____ You go __ march-in' to the ta - ble, ____ You see the same damn

thing, Well it's on ___ one ___ ta - ble, ___ Knife and fork and

pan. ___ And if you say a thing a -

bout it, ___ you're in troub - le with the man. *chorus* Let the mid - night

spe - cial ___ shine its light on me. ___ Let the mid - night

spe - cial, ___ shine her ev - er - lov - ing light on me. __

If you ever go to Houston,
Boy's you better walk right.
And you better not stagger,
And you better not fight.

The sheriff will arrest you,
And he'll carry you down.
And if the jury finds you guilty,
Your penitentiary bound.

chorus

Yonder comes Miss Rosie,
How in the world do you know.
I can tell by her apron,
And the dress she wore.

Umbrella on her shoulder,
Piece of paper in her hand.
She goes a-marching to the captain,
says, "I want my man."

chorus

Georgia Bound

Recorded by: Blind Blake

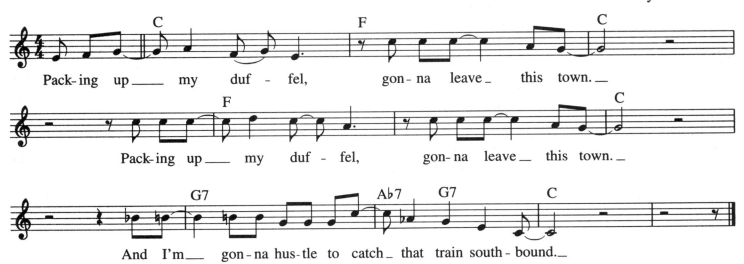

Pack-ing up ___ my duf - fel, gon - na leave ___ this town. ___

Pack-ing up ___ my duf - fel, gon - na leave ___ this town. ___

And I'm ___ gon-na hus-tle to catch ___ that train south - bound. ___

Got the Georgia blues for the plow and hoe.(2X)
Walked out my shoes over this ice and snow.

Tune up the fiddle, dust off the bow.(2X)
Put on the griddle, and open up the cabin door.

I thought I was going to the north land to stay.(2X)
South is on my mind, my blues won't go away.

Potatoes in the ashes, possum on the stove.(2X)
You can have the hash, but leave it on the clove.

Chicken on the roof, babe, watermelons on the vine.(2X)
I'll be glad to get back, to that Georgia gal of mine.

Vicksburg Blues

Recorded by: Little Brother Montgomery

I been wor - ried all day, ma - ma, ___ Mm - mm, ___

And could-n't hard - ly sleep last ___ night. ___

I ___ been wor - ried all day, ma - ma, ___

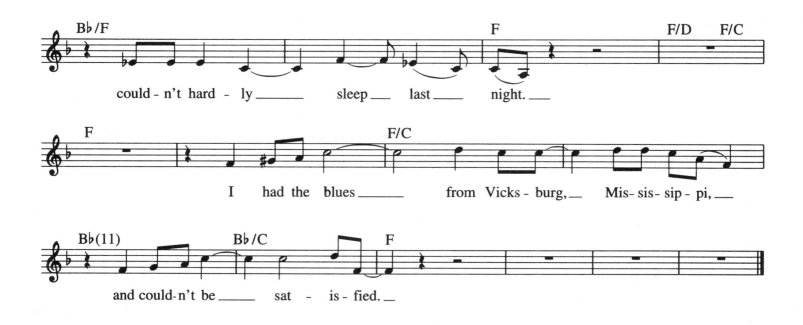

could- n't hard - ly _____ sleep _ last _ night. _

I had the blues _____ from Vicks - burg, _ Mis- sis- sip - pi, _

and could-n't be _____ sat - is - fied. _

Down there is Vicksburg, Mississippi, where I long to be.(2X)
I got a cool pretty mama waiting there for me.

Now there is nothing I can do, Mama, or no more I can say.(2X)
All I know I'm due in Vicksburg, Lord, this very day.

Crow Jane

Recorded by: Big Bill Broonzy
Carl Martin
Brownie McGee
Skip James

Crow Jane, Crow Jane, _ don't hold your head _ so

high, 'Cause _ some- day, _ ba- by, you got to lay down and die. _

I dug her grave with a silver spade,
Ain't nobody gonna take my Crow Jane's place.

You know I let her down with a golden chain,
And every link I would call my Crow Jane's name.

I never missed my water till my well runs dry,
Didn't miss Crow Jane until the day she died.

Crow Jane, Crow Jane, what makes you hold your head so high,
Someday, baby, you're gonna lay down and die.

Police Dog Blues

Recorded by: Blind Arthur Blake

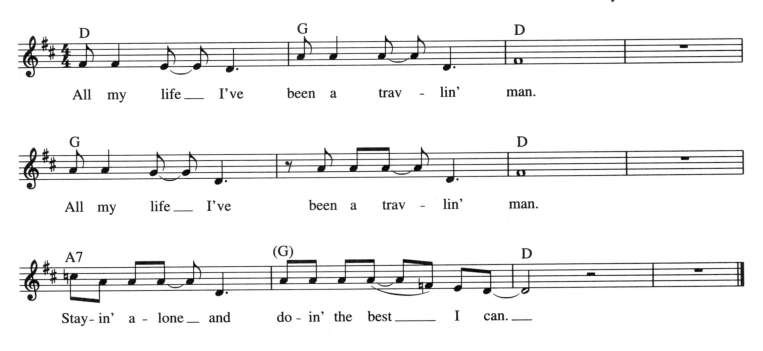

All my life ___ I've been a trav - lin' man.

All my life ___ I've been a trav - lin' man.

Stay - in' a - lone ___ and do - in' the best ___ I can. ___

I shipped my trunk down to Tennessee.(2X)
Hard to tell about a man like me.

I met a gal, I couldn't get her off my mind.(2X)
She passed me up, said she didn't like my kind.

I'm scared to bother around her house at night.(2X)
She got a police dog cravin' for a fight.

His name is Rambler, when he gets a chance.(2X)
He leaves his mark on everybody's pants.

Guess I'll travel, I guess I'll let her be.(2X)
Before she sicks her police dog on me.

Blues Ain't Nothing

Recorded by: Georgia White

Well, the blues ain't noth - in', no, the blues ain't noth - in' but a

good man feel - in' bad. ___ No, the blues ain't noth - in' but a

good man feel - in' bad. It

must have been __ those wear - y blues __ I had. __

Honey, when I die, honey, when I die,
Don't you go wear no black.
Honey, when I die, don't go wear no black,
For if you do, my bones'll come a-creeping back.

I'm a-going downtown, I'm a-going downtown,
Gonna buy myself some glue.
I'm a-going down town, gonna buy myself some glue,
'Cause the woman I've been loving, she broke my heart in two.

Weeping Willow Blues

Recorded by: Blind Boy Fuller

Lord, that weep - in' wil- low, and that mourn - in' dove.

That weep - in' wil- low, and that mourn - in' dove. _____

I got a gal up the coun - try, you know_ I sure __ do love.

Now if you see my woman, tell her I says hurry home.(2X)
I ain't had no loving since my gal been gone.

Where it ain't no love, ain't no getting along.(2X)
My gal treat me so mean and dirty, sometime I don't know right from wrong.

Lord, I lied down last night, tried to take my rest.(2X)
My mind started wandering like the wild geese in the west.

Gonna buy me a bulldog, watch you while I sleep.(2X)
Just to keep these men from making the 'fore day creep.

You gonna want my love, baby, some lonesome day.(2X)
Then it will be too late, I'll be gone too far away.

St. James Infirmary

Recorded by: Josh White

I went down to the St. James In - fir - ma - ry, ___

I saw my ba - by there. ___ Stretched out ___ on a long white

ta - ble, ___ So sweet, ___ so cold, ___ so fair. ___

It was down in old Joe's barroom,
On a corner by the square.
The drinks were served as usual,
And the usual crowd was there.

On my left stood Joe McKennedy,
His eyes were bloodshot red.
He turned to the crowd around him,
These were the words he said:

"Let her go, let her go, God bless her,
Wherever she may be,
She could search this wide world over,
Never find a man as sweet as me.

"When I die please bury me,
In my high-topped Stetson hat.
Put a gold-piece in my watch-farb,
So the gang will know I died standing pat.

"I want six gamblers to be my pallbearers,
Six women to sing me a song.
Put a jazz band on my hearse wagon,
To raise hell as we roll along.

"Now that you heard my story,
I'll take another shot of booze.
And if anybody happens to ask you,
Tell them I got those gambler's blues."

Kansas City Blues

by Jim Jackson

Recorded by: Jim Jackson

Woke up this morn-ing, feel-ing bad, — Thought a-bout the good times I

once have had, — When I lived in Kan-sas Cit-y, _____ When I

lived in Kan-sas Cit-y, _____ I'm gon-na move, ba-by.

where I know they don't __ (a)'llow you. ____

My mama told me, papa told me too,
Brown men and hard liquor gonna be the death of you.
I'm gonna move to Kansas City, gonna move to Kansas City,
Gonna move, baby, where I know they don't know you.

I've got me a bulldog, shepherd, two greyhounds,
Two high yellows, three blacks, one good brown.
We're gonna move to Kansas City, gonna move to Kansas City,
We're gonna move, baby, honey, where they don't know you.

T stands for Texas, T for Tennessee,
Boll Weevil's got Mississippi, and the men are after me.
I'm gonna move to Kansas City, I'm gonna move to Kansas City,
I'm gonna move, baby, honey, where they don't know you.

It takes a rocking chair to rock, rubber ball to roll,
It takes a brownskin man to satisfy my soul.
I'm gonna move to Kansas City, I'm gonna move to Kansas City,
I'm gonna move, baby, honey, where they don't know you.

I love you baby, gonna tell no lie,
The day you quit me, that's the day you'll die.
We're gonna move to Kansas City, we're gonna move to Kansas City,
We're gonna move, baby, honey, where they don't know you.

Got the Blues, Can't Be Satisfied

by Mississippi John Hurt

Recorded by: Mississippi John Hurt

Got the blues, _ can't be sat - is - fied.

Got the blues, __ can't be sat - is - fied. __

Keep the blues, __ I'll catch that train and ride. __

Yes, whiskey straight will drive the blues away.(2X)
That be the case, I wants a quart today.

I bought my baby a great big diamond ring.(2X)
Come right back home and caught her shaking that thing.

I said, "Babe, what make you do me this a-way?"(2X)
Well, that I bought, now you give it away.

I took my gun and broke the barrel down.(2X)
I put that joker six feet in the ground.

You got the blues, and I still ain't satisfied.(2X)
Well, some old day, gonna catch that train and ride.

Rainy Day Blues

by Sam Hopkins and Mack McCormick

Recorded by: Lightning Hopkins

Lord, I'm just sit - tin' down here think - in', _____ what am I gon - na do on this rain - y day? _____ Yes, I'm just sit-tin' down here think - in', _____ what am I gon - na do on this rain - y day? _____ Well, it don't look like the clouds ___ ev - er _____ gon - na let the sun shine an - oth - er day. _____

Yeah, you know if it keeps on raining, old Lightnin' can't make no time.(2X)
Yeah, you know, I can't help but worry about her,
Oh Lord, about that little girl of mine.

They tell me it's raining, that's the time a man has the blues.(2X)
Well, you know I can't be happy, 'cause my baby left me,
She left me my old run down shoes.

Did I tell you what I'm going to do, man, on this rainy day?(2X)
Well, it don't look like the sun is gonna ever shine,
Oh Lord, the cloud won't pass away.

Backwater Blues
by Bessie Smith

Recorded by: Bessie Smith
Leadbelly

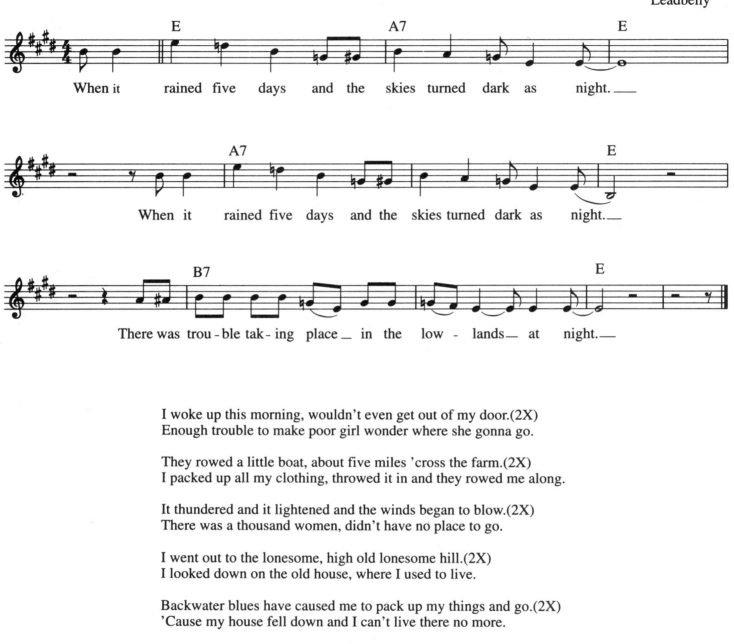

When it rained five days and the skies turned dark as night. ___

When it rained five days and the skies turned dark as night. ___

There was trou-ble tak-ing place ___ in the low-lands ___ at night. ___

I woke up this morning, wouldn't even get out of my door.(2X)
Enough trouble to make poor girl wonder where she gonna go.

They rowed a little boat, about five miles 'cross the farm.(2X)
I packed up all my clothing, throwed it in and they rowed me along.

It thundered and it lightened and the winds began to blow.(2X)
There was a thousand women, didn't have no place to go.

I went out to the lonesome, high old lonesome hill.(2X)
I looked down on the old house, where I used to live.

Backwater blues have caused me to pack up my things and go.(2X)
'Cause my house fell down and I can't live there no more.

Mmm, I can't live there no more.(2X)
And there ain't no place for a poor old girl to go.

That's No Way to Get Along
by Robert Wilkins

Recorded by: Rev. Robert Wilkins

I'm go-in' home, ___ friends, sit down, ___ and tell ___ my, ___ my

These low down women, mama, they treated your, aw, poor son wrong,
Mama, treated me wrong.
These low down women, mama, treated your poor son wrong.(2X`)
And that's no way to get along.

They treated me like my poor heart was made of rock or stone,
Mama, made of a rock or stone.
Treated me like my poor heart was made of a rock or stone.(2X)
And that's no way to get along.

You know, that was enough, mama,to make your son wished he's dead and gone,
Mama, wished I's dead and gone.
That's enough to make your son, mama, wished he's dead and gone.(2X)
'Cause that's no way to get along.

I stood on the roadside, I cried alone, all by myself,
I cried alone by myself.
I stood on the roadside and cried alone by myself.(2X)
Cryin', "that's no way for me to get along."

I's wantin' some train, for some train, to come along and take me away from here,
Friends, take me away from here.
Some train to come along and take me away from here.(2X)
And that's no way for me to get along.

Baby Please Don't Go

by Sam Hopkins

Recorded by: Lightning Hopkins
Big Bill Broonzy
Big Joe Williams

A drone throughout

Ba - by, please don't go. _____ Oh, ba - by,

please don't go. _____ Oh, ba - by, please _ don't go, back to

New Or - leans, _ be - cause I love you so. _____

Turn your lamp down low.(2X)
Turn your lamp down low, 'cause I love you so,
Baby, please don't go.

They got me way down here.(2x)
They got me way down here by the rolling fog,
Treat me like a dog.

Don't call my name.(2X)
Got me way down here, wearing a ball and chain,
Baby please don't go, baby please don't go.

I'm So Glad

by Nehemiah 'Skip' James

Recorded by: Skip James

Fast ♩ = 200

I'm so glad, I'm so glad, I'm

glad, _____ I'm glad. I don't know what to do, _____

don't know what to do, _____ I don't know what _ to do. _____

I'm tired of weep - in', _____ tired _____ of moan- in', _____

tired of groan - in' _____ for you. _____

I'm so tired of moanin', tired of groanin', tired of longin' for you.
I'm so glad, and I am so glad. I am glad, I'm glad.
I don't know what to do, know what to do. I don't know what to do.
I'm so tired, and I am tired. I am tired...

And I'm so glad, I am glad, I am glad, I'm glad.
I don't know what to do, know what to do. I don't know what to do.
I'm tired of weepin', tired of moanin', tired of groanin' for you.
I'm so glad, and I am glad. I'm glad, I'm glad.
I don't know what to do, know what to do. Don't know what to do.

Come Back Baby

Recorded by: Snooks Eaglin
Lightning Hopkins

Please come back, ba - by, _____ please don't go, _____ For the way I

love you, _____ you'll nev - er know. So come back, ba - by, _____ let's talk it

o - ver, _____ just one _____ more time

For the way I love you, you know I do,
For the way you love me, baby,
You never know.
Come back, baby, let's talk it over,
One more time.

You know I love you, tell the world I do,
For the way I love you, baby,
You'll never know.
So come back, baby, let's talk it over,
One more time.

Death Don't Have No Mercy

by Rev. Gary Davis

Recorded by: Rev. Gary Davis

Death don't have no mer-cy, _____ in this land. _____

Death don't _ have no mer-cy, _____ in this land. _____ He

come to your _ house _ and he won't stay long, _ You look in the _ bed _ and some-bod-y

will be gone. _ Death don't _ have _ no mer-cy, _____ in this land. _____

Death never takes a vacation, in this land.
Death never takes a vacation, in this land.
Well, he come to your house and he won't stay long,
You look in the bed and your mother will be gone.
Death never takes a vacation, in this land.

Well, he'll leave you standing and cryin', in this land.
He'll leave you standing and cryin', on this land.
He'll come to your house and he won't stay long,
You look in the bed and somebody will be gone.
He'll leave you standing and crying, in this land.

Oh, death is always in a hurry, in this land.
Death is always in a hurry, in this land.
Well, he'll come to your house and he won't stay long,
You'll look around, and somebody will be gone.
Death is always in a hurry, in this land.

He won't give you time to get ready, in this land.
He won't give you time to get ready, in this land.
Death'll come to your house and he won't stay long,
You look in the bed and somebody will be gone.
He won't give you time to get ready, in this land.

Death will go in any family, in this land.
Death will go in any family, in this land.
He'll come to your house and he won't stay long,
You look in the bed and one of the family will be gone.
Death will go in any family, in this land.

Rev. Gary Davis

That Will Never Happen No More

The wind in Chicago, winter and fall,
Is what caused me to wear my overalls.
Got broke, it was my fault,
Been used to eating porkchops and meat and salt.
I met a woman, just a pigmeat some,
Big fat mouth, me followed her.
She pulled a gun, take my joint,
Didn't leave me hard on, didn't get sore.

chorus

Big Road Blues

Recorded by: Tommy Johnson

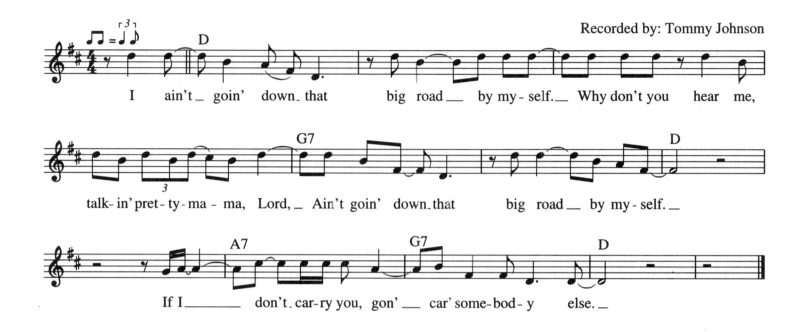

I ain't _ goin' down _ that big road _ by my - self. _ Why don't you hear me,

talk - in' pret - ty - ma - ma, Lord, _ Ain't goin' down _ that big road _ by my - self. _

If I _____ don't _ car-ry you, gon' __ car' some-bod - y else. _

Cryin', sun goin' shine in my back door someday,
Now, don't you hear me talkin', pretty mama, Lord,
Sun goin' to shine in my back door someday.
And the wind goin' to change, goin' to blow my blues away.

Baby, what makes you do, like you do, do, do, like you do, do, do,
Don't you hear me now,
What makes you do me, like you do, do, do.
Now you say you goin' to do me like you done poor Cherry Red.

Bad Luck Blues

Recorded by: Blind Lemon Jefferson

I want to go __ home,__ but I ain't __ got suf-fi-cient clothes__ __ dog-gone __ my bad __ luck soul.__ Want to go home,__ and I __ ain't __ __ got suf-fi-cient clothes.__ I mean suf-fi-cient, talkin' 'bout soul, __ I want__ __ to go __ home,__ But I ain't __ got suf-fi-cient clothes, __

I bet my money and I lost it, Lord,
Doggone my bad luck soul,
Mmm, lost a great big roll,
I mean lost it, speaking about dough, now.
I'll never bet on this old trey game no more.

Oh, my big gal has gone. why don't you quit your cryin',
Doggone my bad luck soul,
Mmm, why don't you quit your cryin',
Why don't you quit, I mean cryin'.
That joker stole off with that long-haired brown of mine.

Sister, catch the Katy, I'll catch that Santa Fe,
Doggone my bad luck soul,
Sister, you catch the Katy, I'll catch that Santa Fe,
I mean Santa, speaking about Fe.
When you get to Denver, pretty mama, look around for me.

The woman I love is five feet from the ground,
Doggone my bad luck soul,
Hey, five feet from the ground.
Five feet from the, I mean ground.
She's a tailor made woman, she ain't no hand-me-down.

I ain't seen my sugar in two long weeks today,
Doggone my bad luck soul,
Seen my sugar in two long weeks today,
Two long weeks, I mean 'day.
Girl, it's been so long, seems like my heart's gonna break.

I'm gonna run 'cross town, catch that southbound Santy Fe,
Doggone my bad luck soul,
Mmm, Lord, that Santy Fe,
I mean Santy, singing about Fe.
Be on my to what you call loving Tennessee.

Big Bill Broonzy

Searching the Desert
For the Blues

Recorded by: Blind Willie McTell

You may search ___ the o - cean, ___ you might

go 'cross the deep blue ___ sea. _____ But ma - ma, you'll nev - er find, an -

oth - er hot shot ___ like me. _____

I follow my baby from the station to the train,
And the blues came down like night and showered me.

I left her at the station wringing her hands and crying,
I told her she had a home, just as long as I had mine.

I've got two woman, and you can't tell them apart,
I got one in my bosom, and one I got in my heart.

San Francisco Bay Blues

Words and Music by Jesse Fuller

Recorded by: Jesse Fuller

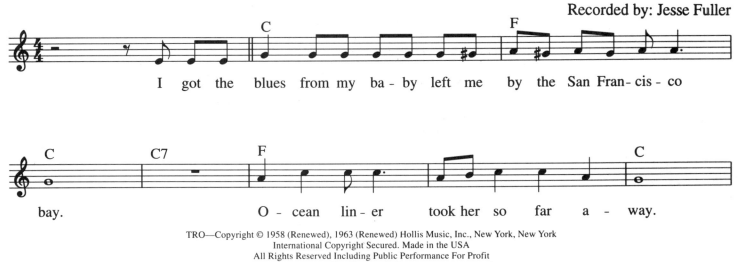

I got the blues from my ba - by left me by the San Fran - cis - co

bay. O - cean lin - er took her so far a - way.

Did-n't mean to treat her so bad, ___ she was the best gal I ev - er

had, _____ Said good - bye, _____ made me cry, _____

I want to lay down and die. ___ I ain't got a nick - el and I

ain't got a lous - y dime. She ev - er come back, I

think I'm gon - na loose my mind, _ If she ev - er comes back to

stay, It will be an - oth - er brand new day, _____

Walk-in' with my ba - by down by the San Fran- cis - co bay. _____

Sitting down by my back door, wondering which way to go,
Woman I'm so crazy about, she don't love me no more.
Think I'll take me a freight train, 'cause I'm feeling blue,
Ride all the way till the end of the line, thinking only of you.

Meanwhile, in another city, just about to go insane,
Sound like I heard my baby, the way she used to call my name.
If she ever come back to stay, it will be another brand new day,
Walking with my baby down by the San Francisco Bay.

Sitting on Top of the World

Recorded by: Mississippi Sheiks

Was in the spring, one summer day,
Just when she left me, she thought she'd stay.
But now she's gone, I don't worry,
I'm sitting on top of the world.

(Didn't you) Come here running, holding out you hand,
Can't get me a woman, quicker than you can get a man.
But now she's gone, I don't worry,
I'm sitting on top of the world.

It has been days, didn't know your name,
Why should I worry myself in vain.
But now she's gone, I don't worry,
I'm sitting on top of the world.

Went to the station, down in the yard,
Gon' get me a freight train, work's done got hard.
But now she's gone, I don't worry,
I'm sitting on top of the world.

The lonesome days, they have gone by,
Why should you beg me, and say goodbye.
But now she's gone, I don't worry,
I'm sitting on top of the world.

That's All Right
Mama

by Arthur Big Boy Crudup

Recorded by: Arthur Crudup
Elvis Presley

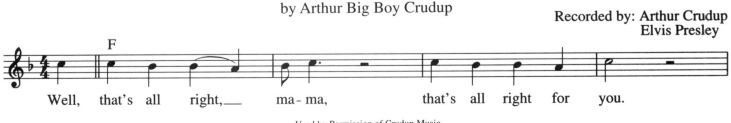

That's all right __ ma - ma, just __ an - y way you do. That's all right,

that's all right, __ That's all right ____ ma - ma, __

an - y way you __ do.

My mama she done told me, pap's done told me too,
Son, that gal you're foolin' with, she ain't no good for you.
But that's all right, that's all right,
That's all right, mama, any way you do.

I'm leaving town tomorrow, leaving town for sure.
Then you won't be bothered with me hanging 'round your door.
But that's all right, that's all right,
That's all right, mama, any way you do.

I oughtta mind my pap, guess I'm not too smart.
If I was I'd leave you, go before you break my heart.
But that's all right, that's all right,
That's alright, mama, any way you do.

You Got to Move

by Fred McDowell and Gary Harding Davis

Recorded by: Fred McDowell

D modal tonality throughout

You got to move, you _ got to move, You got to move (child), __ you got to

move, But when the Lord _ get read - y, _____ you got to move. __

You may be high, you may be low,
You may be rich, child, you may be poor,
But when the Lord gets ready, you got to move.

You see that woman that walks the street?
You see that policeman out on his beat?
But when the Lord gets ready, you got to move.

Bulldoze Blues
Going Up the Country

Recorded by: Henry Thomas

I'm goin'_ a - way,_ babe,　and it won't_ be _ long. _

I'm　go - in' a - way,_　and it　won't_ be　long. _

I'm _　goin'　away _____ and it　won't_ be　long. _

Just as soon as that train is out of that Mobile yard.(3X)

I'll shake your hand, tell your bible goodbye.(3X)

I'm going back to Memphis, Tennessee.(3X)

I'm goin' where I never get the blues.(3X)

If you don't think I'm sinkin', look what a hole I'm in.(2X)
If you don't believe I'm sinkin', look what a fool I been.

Oh, my babe, take me back.(2X)
How in the world, goin' to take me back.

Woke Up This Morning

by B.B. King and Jule Taub

Recorded by: B.B. King

Rhumba feel

I woke up this morn-in', my ba - by was gone.

(I) woke up this morn - in', my ba - by was gone.

I feel so bad, I'm all a - lone.

I ain't got nobody, stayin' home with me.(2X)
My baby, she's gone, I'm in misery.

Hey babe, I'm all alone.(2X)
I ain't had no lovin', my baby been gone.

Mississippi John Hurt

Brown's Ferry Blues

Recorded by: Doc Watson

Half time feel

Hard luck pal, com - in' down the lane,

Ma - ma give him back his walk - in' cane, Lord, Lord, __ I got them

Brown's Fer - ry blues. ___ Throwed it a - way and he

went to town, __ see that wom - an and now he's down,

Lord, Lord, __ I got them Brown's Fer - ry blues. ___

Hard luck papa, gettin' too tight,
If he don't quit drinking, he'll be high as a kite,
Lord, Lord, got those Brown's Ferry blues.
He'd been drinkin' that block and tackle kind,
He can walk a block and tackle that line,
Lord, Lord, got them Brown's Ferry blues.

Hard luck papa standing in the rain,
If the world was corn, he couldn't buy grain,
Lord, Lord, got them Brown's Ferry blues.
He runs around in second hand clothes,
You can smell his feet where ever he goes,
Lord, Lord, I got them Brown's Ferry blues.

Revenue man took my gin,
I hope they won't come back again,
Lord, Lord, got them Brown's Ferry blues.
Took my sweetie with him too,
'Cause she had a little drink or two,
Lord, Lord, I got them Brown's Ferry blues.

Deep River Blues

by Doc Watson

Recorded by: DocWatson

Let it rain, ___ let it pour, ___ Let it ___ rain ___ a whole lot more, ___ 'Cause I got them Deep Riv- er blues. ___

Let the rain ___ drive right on, ___ Let the waves ___ sweep a - long, ___ 'Cause I got ___ those Deep Riv- er blues. _____

My old gal's a good old pal,
And she looks like a water fowl,
When I get them Deep River blues.

There ain't no one to cry for me,
And the fish all go out on a spree,
When I get them Deep River blues.

Give me back my old boat,
I'm gonna sail if she float,
'Cause I got them Deep River blues.

I'm goin' back to Muscle Shoals,
Times are better there, I'm told,
'Cause I got them Deep River blues.

If my boat sinks with me,
I'll go down don't you see,
'Cause I got them Deep River blues.

Now I'm gonna say goodbye,
And if I sink just let me die,
'Cause I got them Deep River blues.

St. Louis Blues

Recorded by: Bessie Smith
Ida Cox

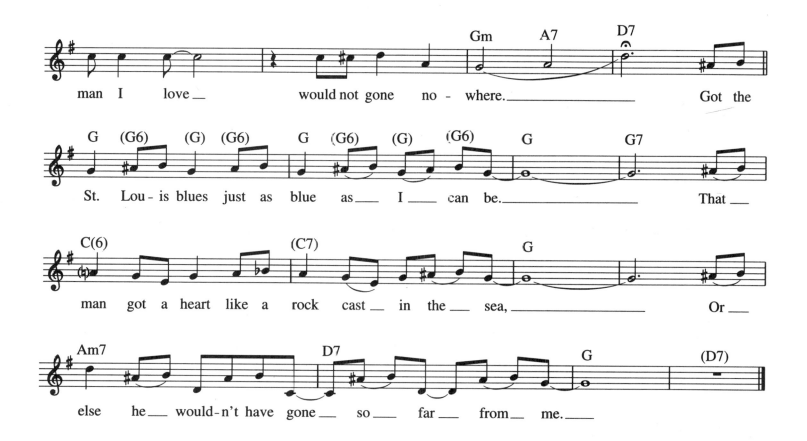

man I love — would not gone no - where. _____ Got the

St. Lou - is blues just as blue as __ I __ can be. _____ That __

man got a heart like a rock cast __ in the __ sea, _____ Or __

else he __ would-n't have gone __ so __ far __ from __ me. __

2. Been to the Gypsy to get my fortune told,
   To the Gypsy, to get my fortune told.
   'Cause I'm most wild about my jelly roll.

   Gypsy done told me: "Don't you wear no black,"
   Yes she done told me: "Don't you wear no black,"
   Go to St. Louis, you can win him back.

   Help me to Cairo, make St. Louis by myself,
   Gone to Cairo, find my old friend Jeff.
   Goin' to pin myself close to his side,
   If I flag his train, I sure can ride.

   I love that man like a schoolboy loves his pie,
   Like a Kentucky Colonel loves his mint and rye.
   I'll love my baby till the day I die.

3. You ought to see that stovepipe brown of mine,
   Like he owns the diamond Joseph line.
   He'd make a cross-eyed old man go stone blind.

   Blacker than midnight, teeth like flags of truce,
   Blackest man in the whole St. Louis.
   Blacker the berry, sweeter is the juice.

   About a crap game, he knows a powerful lot,
   But when work time comes, he's on the dot,
   Goin' to ask him for a cold ten spot,
   What it takes to get it, he's certainly got.

   A black-headed gal make a freight train jump the track,
   Said a black-headed gal make a freight train jump the track.
   But a red-headed woman makes a preacher ball the jack.

Baby What You Want Me to Do

by Jimmy Reed

Recorded by: Jimmy Reed

vocal harmony in top voice

Got me run - nin', __ you got me hid - in', __ You got me

run, hide, hide, run, an - y way you want to, Let it roll,

yeah, _____ yeah, yeah, _____ You got me

doin' what you want me, __ Ba - by, why you want to let go? __

Goin' up, goin' down,
Goin' up, down, down, up, any way you want it,
Let it roll, yeah, yeah, yeah,
You got me doin' what you want me,
Baby, why you want to let it go?

Got me beeping, got me hiding,
Got me beep, hide, hide, beep, any way you want to,
Let it roll, yeah, yeah, yeah,
You got me doin' what you want,
Baby, why you want to let it go?

Don't Fish in My Sea

Recorded by: Ma Rainey

My dad - dy come home this morn - nin', drunk as he ___ could

be.

My dad - dy come home this morn - nin',

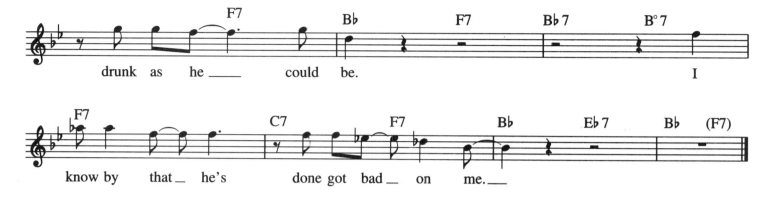

drunk as he ____ could be.   I

know by that __ he's   done got bad __ on me. __

He used to stay out late, now he don't come home at all.(2X)
I know there's another mule been kicking in my stall.

If you don't like my ocean, don't fish in my sea.(2X)
Stay out of my valley, let my mountain be.

I ain't had no loving since God knows when.(2X)
That's the reason I'm through with these no-good, trifling men.

You'll never miss the sunshine till the rain begin to fall.(2X)
You'll never miss you ham till another mule be in your stall.

Bright Lights, Big City

by Jimmy Reed

vocal harmony in top voice

Recorded by: Jimmy Reed

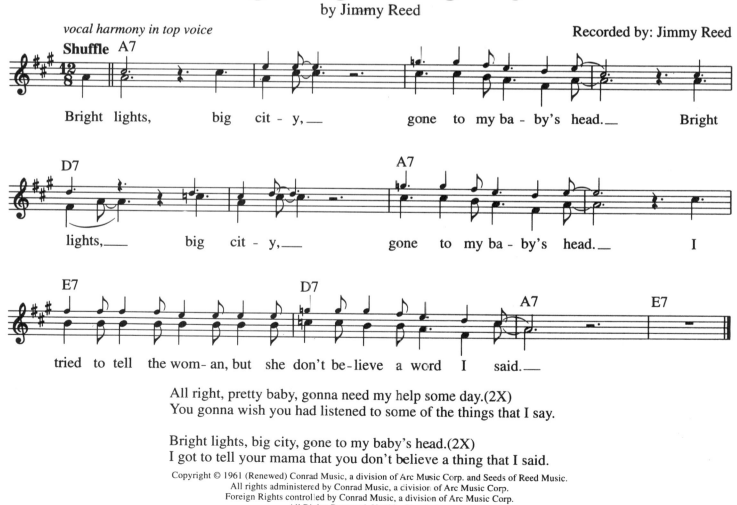

Bright lights,   big cit - y, ____   gone to my ba - by's head. __   Bright

lights, ____   big cit - y, ____   gone to my ba - by's head. __   I

tried to tell the wom- an, but she don't be-lieve a word I said. __

All right, pretty baby, gonna need my help some day.(2X)
You gonna wish you had listened to some of the things that I say.

Bright lights, big city, gone to my baby's head.(2X)
I got to tell your mama that you don't believe a thing that I said.

Mean Old Frisco

by Arthur 'Big Boy' Crudup

Recorded by: Arthur Crudup

Fast

F7

Well, that mean ___ old, mean old Fris - co, ___

and than low ___ down San - ta Fe. Well, that mean old

Bb 7

Fris - co, and that low down San - ta Fe. ___

C7

Well, it car-ried my babe a way, _____

(Bb 7)

F7   (C7)   F7

And it's blown right back on me. ___

I was standing, I was listening, for that Southern whistle to blow.
I was standing and listening for that Southern whistle to blow.
Lord, she did not catch the Southern,
And now where do you suppose that woman might have gone?

Well, then I ain't, I ain't got no, got no special rider here, Lord.
I ain't got no special rider here.
Well, I think I will leave,
'Cause I don't feel welcome.

Well, my mama she done told me, and my papa told me, too.
Well, my mama she done told me, and my papa told me, too.
Everybody grins in your face son,
Well, they ain't no friend of yours.

Born Under a Bad Sign

by Booker T. Jones and William Bell

Recorded by: Albert King
Booker T.

I can't read, I didn't learn how to write.
My whole life has been one big fight.

chorus

You know, wine and women is all I crave.
A big legged woman gon' carry me to my grave.

chorus

Jailhouse Blues

by Bessie Smith and Clarence Williams

Recorded by: Bessie Smith

Thir-ty days in jail, with my back turned to the wall, to the wall. Thir-ty days in jail, with my back turned to the wall. Look here, mis-ter jail keep-er, put an-oth-er gal in my stall.

I don't mind being in jail, but I got to stay there so long, so long.(2X)
Well, every friend I had has done shook hands and gone.

You better stop you man from ticklin' me under my chin, under my chin.
You better stop your man from ticklin' me under my chin.
'Cause if he keeps on ticklin', I'm sure gonna take him on in.

Good morning blues, blues how do you do? How do you do?
Good morning blues, blues how do you do?
Well, I just come here to have a few words with you.

Good Morning Little Schoolgirl

by Sonny Boy Williamson

Recorded by: Sonny Boy Williamson
Muddy Waters
Junior Wells

Good morn - ing lit - tle school girl, good morn - ing lit - tle school girl, Can I go home with, can I go

home ___ with you?   Tell your

moth-er ___ and your fath-er, ___   I once was a school boy too.

Sometime I don't know what, sometime I don't know what,
Woman, what in this world to, woman, what in this world to do.
I don't want to hurt your feeling, or either get mad at you.

I'm gonna buy me an airplane, I'm gonna buy me an airplane,
I'm gonna fly all over shanty town.
If I don't find my baby, I ain't gonna let my airplane down.

Now who's that comin' yonder? Now who's that comin' yonder?
She's all dressed up in pretty, she's dressed up in pretty red.
If she don't be my baby, I'd sooner see her dead.

Stormy Monday

Written by T. Bone Walker

Recorded by: T. Bone Walker

They call it storm-y Mon - day, ___   but Tues-day's just as bad. ___

They call it storm - y Mon ___ day, _____   but Tues - day's just as bad._

___   Wednes-day's worse,

and ___ Thurs-day's al - so sad. ___

Yes, the eagle flies on Friday, and Saturday I go out to play.(2X)
Sunday I go to church, then I kneel down and pray.

Lord have mercy, Lord have mercy on me.
Lord have mercy, my heart's in misery.
Crazy 'bout my baby, yes, send her back to me.

The Thrill is Gone

by B.B. King and Joe Josea

Recorded by: B.B. King

The thrill is gone, _ the thrill is gone _ a way.

The thrill is gone _____ ba - by, the thrill is gone _____

_ a - way. _ You know you done me wrong _____ _ ba - by,

_ and you'll be sor - ry some day. _____

The thrill is gone, it's gone away from me.(2X)
Although I'll still live on, but so lonely I'll be.

The thrill is gone, it's gone away for good.(2X)
Someday I know I'll be over it all, baby, just like I know a good man should.

You know I'm free, free now, baby, I'm free from your spell.(2X)
And now that it's all over, all I can do is wish you well.

Built for Comfort

by Willie Dixon

Recorded by: Willie Dixon

Some folk(s) built like this, _ some folk(s) built like that, _ But the

way I'm built (a) don't you call me fat, _ Be-cause I'm built _ for com - fort, _

I — ain't — built for speed. — But I got ev-er-y-thing, All — that a good girl needs. —

I ain't got no diamonds, I ain't got no boat,
But I do have love that's gonna fire your soul,
'Cause I'm built for comfort, I ain't built for speed.
But I got everything, all you good women need.

Sweet Little Angel

by B.B. King and Jules Taub

Recorded by: B.B. King

I've got a sweet lit-tle an-gel. I love — the way — she — spreads her wings. —

— (Yes) Got a sweet lit-tle an — gel —

I love — the way _____ she spreads her wings. —

(Yes) _____ When she spreads her wings — a-round me,

I get joy _____ in eve-ry-thing. _____

You know, I asked my baby for a nickel, and she gave me a twenty dollar bill.
Oh yes, I asked my baby for a nickel, and she gave me a twenty dollar bill.
Well, you know I asked her for a little drink of liquor,
And she gave me a whiskey still.

If my baby was to quit me, well I do believe I would die.
If my baby was to quit me, I do believe I would die.
Yes, if you love me sweet little angel,
Please tell me the reason why.

Alabama Bound

New Words and New Music Adaptation by Huddie Ledbetter

Recorded by: Leadbelly

I'm Al-a-bam-a bound. _ I'm Al-a-bam-a bound. _ I'm Al-a-bam-a bound, _ Al-a-bam-a bound, _ And if the train don't turn a-round, _ I'm Al-a-bam-a bound, _ I'm Al-a-ba-ma bound. _

Oh, don't you leave me here.(2X)
If you will go anyhow, leave a dime for beer.

chorus

Elder Green is gone.(2X)
She is way 'cross the country, sweet gal, with her long clothes on.

chorus

Oh, the preacher preached, the sister turned around,
The deacon's in the corner hollering, "sweet gal, I'm Alabama bound."

chorus

Preacher's in the stand, passin' his hat around,
Sayin', "Brothers and sisters, shoot your money to me, I'm Alabama bound."

chorus

Rock Me Baby

Recorded by: B.B. King

Rock me ba-by, rock me all night long. _

Rock me ba-by, rock me all night long. _

I want you to rock me ba - by, like my back ain't got no bone. ___

Roll me ba - by, like you roll a wag - on wheel.

Roll me ba - by, like you roll a wag - on wheel. I want you to

roll me ba - by, ___ you don't know how it makes me feel.

Rock me baby, honey rock me slow.(2X)
Rock me baby, till I want no more.

Roll me baby, like you roll a wagon wheel.(2X)
I want you to roll me baby, you don't know how it makes me feel.

Hey Hey

Words and Music by Big Bill Broonzy

Recorded by: Big Bill Broonzy

Hey hey, ___ hey hey, ___ ba - by hey. ___

Hey hey, ___ hey hey, ___ ba - by hey. ___

I love you, ba - by, ain't gon - na be your dog. ___

Hey hey, hey hey, baby hey.(2X)
My arms around you, baby, all I can say is hey.

Hey hey, hey hey, baby hey.(2X)
Love you, baby, but I sure ain't gonna be your dog.

Hey hey, lost your good thing now.(2X)
It had me fooled, I found it out somehow.

Sweet Sixteen

by B.B. King and Joe Josea

Recorded by: B.B. King

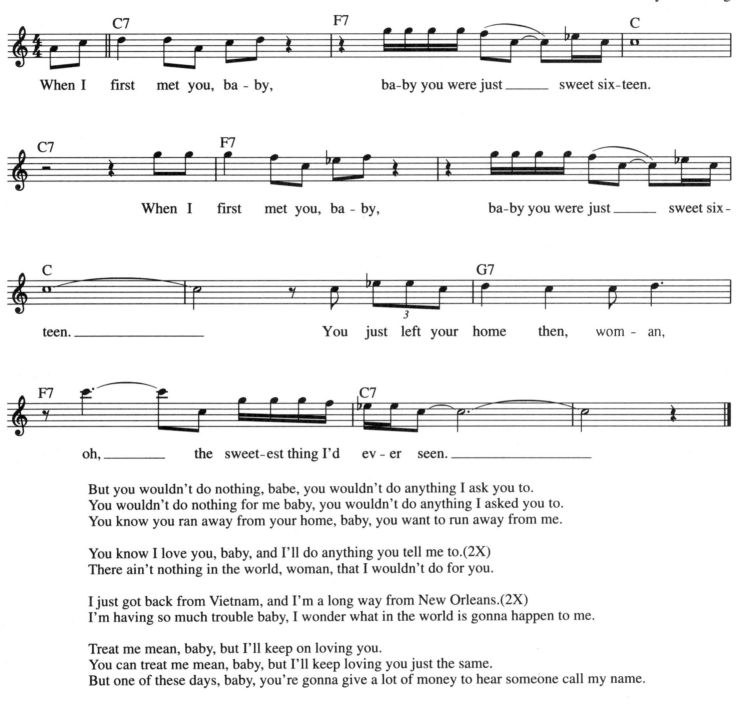

When I first met you, ba - by, ba-by you were just _____ sweet six-teen.

When I first met you, ba - by, ba-by you were just _____ sweet six-

teen. _____ You just left your home then, wom - an,

oh, _____ the sweet-est thing I'd ev - er seen. _____

But you wouldn't do nothing, babe, you wouldn't do anything I ask you to.
You wouldn't do nothing for me baby, you wouldn't do anything I asked you to.
You know you ran away from your home, baby, you want to run away from me.

You know I love you, baby, and I'll do anything you tell me to.(2X)
There ain't nothing in the world, woman, that I wouldn't do for you.

I just got back from Vietnam, and I'm a long way from New Orleans.(2X)
I'm having so much trouble baby, I wonder what in the world is gonna happen to me.

Treat me mean, baby, but I'll keep on loving you.
You can treat me mean, baby, but I'll keep loving you just the same.
But one of these days, baby, you're gonna give a lot of money to hear someone call my name.

Hoochie Coochie Man

by Willie Dixon

Recorded by: Willie Dixon

The gyp-sy wom-an told my moth-er, be-fore I was born: "You got a boy child com-in', goin' be a son of a gun." Gon-na make pret-ty wom-en jump and shout, Then the world gon-na know what it's all a-bout I'm him, Eve-ry-bod-y knows I'm him. I'm the hooch-ie cooch-ie man, Eve-ry-bod-y knows I'm him.

I got a black cat bone,
I got a mojo too,
I got the Johnny conkeroo,
I'm gonna mess with you.
I'm gonna make you girls,
Lead me by my hand,
Then the world's gonna know,
I'm that hoochie coochie man,

chorus

On the seventh hour,
On the seventh day,
On the seventh month,
The seventh doctor said:
"He was born for good luck,"
And that, you'll see,
I got seven hundred dollars,
Don't you mess with me.

chorus

64

Spoonful
by Willie Dixon

Recorded by: Willie Dixon
Muddy Waters
Howlin' Wolf

vamp throughout

It could be a spoon-ful of dia-monds,_ could be a spoon-ful of gold,

Just a lit-tle spoon of your pre - cious love,_ sat - is - fy_ my soul._ Men

lie ___ a-bout a lit-tle, Some men cries ___ a-bout a, Some of ('em)

dies ___ a-bout a lit-tle, Ev' - ry-thing fight a-bout (a)
(one)

spoon - ful,_ That spoon, that spoon, that spoon - ful._

It could be a spoonful of coffee, it could be a spoonful of tea,
But a little spoon of your precious love is good enough for me.

Men lies about that (spoonful),
Some of them dies about that (spoonful),
Some of them cries about that (spoonful),
But everybody fight about that spoonful,
That spoon, that spoon, that spoonful.

It could be a spoonful of water, saved from the desert sand,
But one spoon of luck from my little forty five, save from another man.

You Can't Judge a Book by its Cover
by Willie Dixon

Recorded by: Willie Dixon

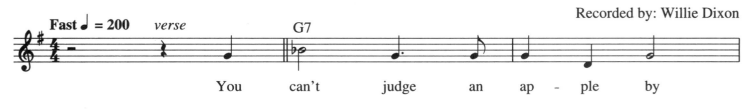

Fast ♩ = 200 *verse* G7

You can't judge an ap - ple by

You can't judge sugar by looking at the cane.
You can't judge a woman by looking at her man.
You can't judge a sister by looking at her brother.
You can't judge a book by looking at the cover.

chorus

You can't judge a fish by looking in the pond.
You can't judge right from looking at the wrong.
You can't judge one by looking at the other.
You can't judge a book by looking at the cover.

chorus

Everyday
I Have the Blues

by Peter Chatman

Recorded by: B.B. King

Eve - ry day, eve - ry day I have the blues. ___

Oh, ___ eve - ry day, ___ eve - ry day I have ___ the blues. ___

___ When you see me worry - in', babe,

and ___ it's you I hate ___ to lose.

Nobody loves me, nobody seems to care.(2X)
Speakin' of worries and troubles, darlin',
You know I've had my share.

Everyday, everyday, everyday, everyday,
Everyday, everyday I have the Blues.
When you see me worryin', woman,
Honey, it's you I hate to lose.

Mellow Down Easy

by Willie Dixon

Recorded by: Willie Dixon

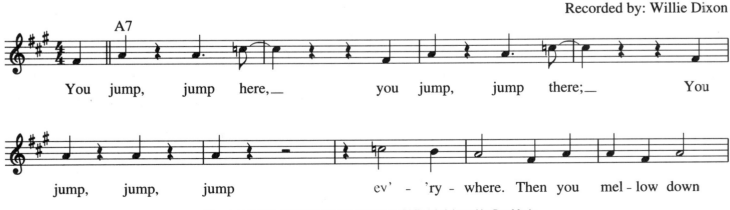

You jump, jump here, ___ you jump, jump there; ___ You

jump, jump, jump ev' - 'ry - where. Then you mel - low down

eas - y,   Mel - low down   eas - y.

(E7)   A7

Mel-low down eas-y when you real-ly want to blow your top._____

Shake, shake here; shake, shake there;
You shake, shake, shake, everywhere.
Then you mellow down easy, mellow down easy.
You mellow down easy when you really want to blow your top.

You wiggle, wiggle here; you wiggle, wiggle there;
You wiggle, wiggle, wiggle, everywhere.
Then you mellow down easy, mellow down easy.
You mellow down easy when you really want to blow your top.

Mary Had a Little Lamb

Recorded by: Buddy Guy

Ma - ry had a lit - tle lamb,__   his fleece was white as __ snow._

__   Eve - ry - where the child   went,

the lamb was sure to __ go._____   He fol - lowed her to   school _

__ one day,   and broke the teach- er's   rule, __

And what a time_(did) they   have ____   that day at   school._

Tisket, tasket, a green a yellow basket,
Sent a letter to my baby,
And on my way I passed it.

Three O'clock Blues

by B.B. King and Jules Taub

Recorded by: B.B. King

Now, here it is, three o'- clock in the morn - ing,___ and I can't ev-en close my ____

___ eyes. ___ Oh yes, it's three o'- clock in the morn - ing ba - by, ___

I ____ can't ev - en close my eyes. ___ Well, I

can't find ___ my ba - by, ___ Lord, ___ and I can't be sat - is - fied. ___

I've looked around me, people, and my baby knows she can't be found.(2X)
Well, you know if I don't find my baby, I'm goin' down to the Golden Ground.

Goodbye everybody, I believe this is the end.(2X)
I want you to tell my baby to forgive me for my sins.

I Just Want to Make Love to You

by Willie Dixon

I don't want_ you to be no slave, ___ I don't want_ you

(to) work all day, ___ I don't want_ you to be true. ___

I just want to make love to you. I don't want_ you to

wash my clothes, ___ I don't want_ you (to) keep our home, ___

I don't want_ your mon- ey too.___ I just want to make love to you.

I don't want you to cook my bread,
I don't want you to make my bed,
I don't want you 'cause I'm sad and blue.
I just want to make love to you.

The Sky is Crying

by Morris Levy, Elmore James and Clarence Lewis

Recorded by: Elmore James

The sky is cryin', look at the tears roll down the street. ___

The sky is cry- in', ___ look at the tears roll down the

street. ___ I been look- ing for my ba - by, _

_ and I won- der where can she be. ___

I saw my baby early one morning, she was walking on down the street.(2X)
You know it hurt me so bad, it made my poor heart skip a beat.

I got a bad feelin', my baby don't love me no more.(2X)
You know the sky is cryin', the tears rolling down my nose.

I Ain't Got Nobody

Recorded by: Bessie Smith

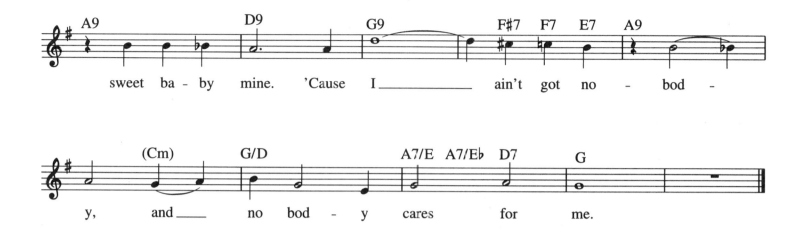

sweet ba - by mine. 'Cause I_____ ain't got no - bod -

y, and____ no bod - y cares for me.

Won't somebody go and find my man and bring him back to me.
It's awful hard to be alone and without sympathy.
Once I was a loving gal, as good as any in this town.
But since my daddy left me, I'm a gal with her heart bowed down.

How Long Blues

Recorded by: Leroy Carr
Skip James

How long, ___ how long, ___ has that eve - nin' train been

gone? How long, _ how long, _ ba - by how long?_

If I could holler like a mountain Jack,
I'd holler and call my baby back.
How long, how long, baby, how long?

How long, how long,
Has that evening train been gone?
How long, how long, baby, how long?

You don't believe I'm sinkin', look what a hole I'm in,
You don't believe me, baby, look what a fool I been.
How long, how long, baby, how long?

Wild About That Thing

Recorded by: Bessie Smith

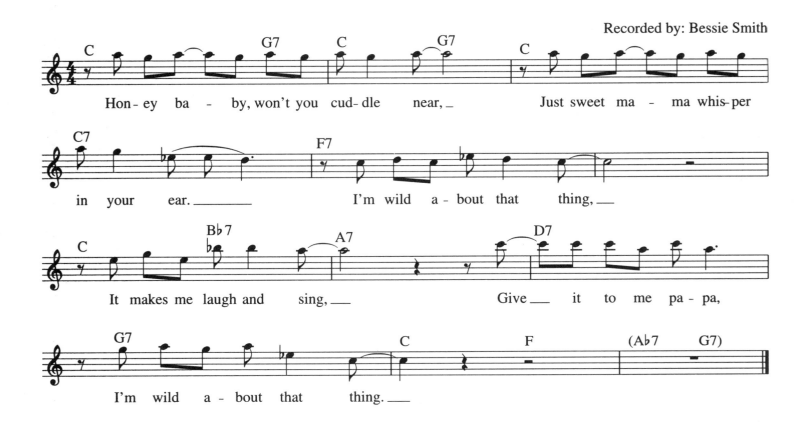

Do it easy, honey, don't get rough,
From you, papa, I can't get enough.
I'm wild about that thing, I'm wild about that thing,
Everybody knows it, I'm wild about that thing.

Please don't hold it, baby, when I cry,
Give me every bit of it or else I'll die.
I'm wild about that thing, ja da ging ging ging,
All the time I'm cryin', I'm wild about that thing.

What's the matter, papa, please don't stop,
Don't you know I love it and I want it all?
I'm wild about that thing, just give my bell a ring,
You touched my button, I'm wild about that thing.

If you want to satisfy my soul,
Come on and rock me with a steady roll.
I'm wild about that thing, gee I like your ting-a-ling.
Kiss me like you mean it, I'm wild about that thing.

Come on turn the lights down low,
Say you're ready, just say let's go.
I'm wild about that thing, I'm wild about that thing,
Come on and make me feel it, I'm wild about that thing.

I'm wild about it when you hold me tight,
Let me linger in your arms all night.
I'm wild about that thing, my passions got the fling,
Come on, hear me cryin', I'm wild about that thing.

Sorrowful Blues

Recorded by: Bessie Smith

If you catch me steal-in', I _____ don't mean no harm. If you

catch _____ me steal-in', I don't mean no harm. It's a

mark in my fam-'ly and it must be car-ryin' on. _____

I got nineteen men and won't want more.(2X)
If I had one more I'd let that nineteen go.

It's hard to love another woman's man.(2X)
You catch him when you want him, you got to catch him when you can.

Have you ever seen a preacher throw a sweet potato pie?(2X)
Just step in my backyard and taste a piece of mine.

I'm gonna tell you, daddy, like Solomon told the Jew.(2X)
If you don't like-ee me, I sure don't like-ee you.

Elizabeth Cotton

T.Bone Shuffle

Recorded by: T. Bone Walker

intro (guitar & horns)

Let your hair down ba - by and let's have a nat - 'ral ball. _____ Let your hair down ba - by, let's have a nat - 'ral ball. _____ 'Cause when your not hap - py, it ain't no fun at all. _____

You can't take it with you, that's one thing for sure.(2X)
There's nothing wrong with you that a good chunk of boogie won't cure.

Have your fun while you can, fate's an awful thing.(2X)
You can't tell what might happen, that's why I love to sing.

See That My Grave is Kept Clean
One Kind Favor

by Blind Lemon Jefferson

Recorded by: Blind Lemon Jefferson

Well,_ it's one kind fa- vor I'll ask of you. _

Well,_ it's one kind fa- vor I'll ask of you.

Lord,_ it's one kind fa- vor _____ I'll ask ___ of

you. Please see _____ that my grave _ is kept clean. _

Two white horses in a line.(2X)
Well, it's two white horses in a line.
Gonna take me to my burying ground.

My heart stop beating, my hands got cold.(3X)
It ain't no more to you but the cypress grove.

Have you ever heard a coffin sound?(3X)
Then you know a poor boy's in the ground.

Dig my grave with silver spade.(3X)
You may lead me down with a hoe and a spade.

Have you ever heard the churchbell toll?(3x)
Then you know a poor boy's dead and gone.

Big Mama Thornton

Cocaine Blues

by Rev. Gary Davis

Recorded by: Rev. Gary Davis

Down to Fourth Street, o - ver to Main, _ Look-in' for the gal that sells co - caine. _

Co - caine, _ run - nin' all ____ 'round _ my brain. _

Come here ma- ma, come here quick, This old co- caine 'bout to make me sick.

Co - caine, _ run - nin' all 'round _ my brain. _

Woke up one morning just about half past four,
Heard somebody knocking on my door.
Cocaine done got all around my brain.

I come in one morning about half past ten,
My gal got a chair tried to do her best to knock me in.
Cocaine done got all around my brain.

Found myself sittin' on the side of the road,
Just spent all the money I had for my room and board.
Cocaine done got all around my brain.

Run here, mama, run here quick,
This cocaine's about to make me sick.
Cocaine done got all around my brain

Woke up this morning about half past six,
My gal done quit me, she done had got me fixed.
Cocaine done got all around my brain.

I said, run here somebody, won't you please run in a hurry,
This cocaine has got me sick.
Cocaine done got all around my brain.

Sometimes I Wonder

Recorded by: Otis Spann

Some-times I won-der, but I ain't got to won-der no more.

Some-time I won-der, but I ain't got to won-der no

more. You know I found me a wom-an

and the lit-tle girl she live next door.

My baby come home this morning, say she had a nice time.(2X)
I asked my baby what was on her worried mind.

If I don't go crazy, baby, I'm gonna lose my mind.(2X)
I'm in love with you woman, keep me bothered all the time.

Hesitation Blues

New Words and Music by Rev. Gary Davis

Recorded by: Rev. Gary Davis

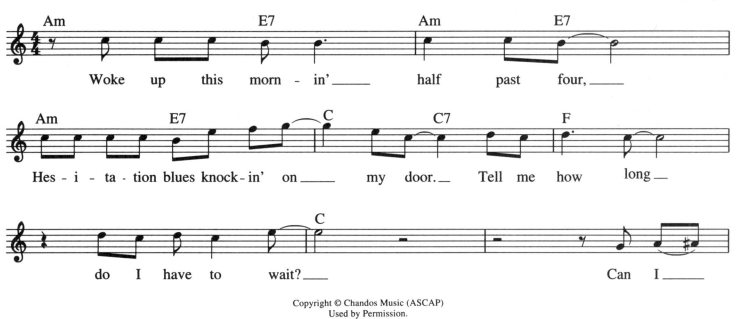

Woke up this morn-in' half past four,

Hes-i-ta-tion blues knock-in' on my door. Tell me how long

do I have to wait? Can I

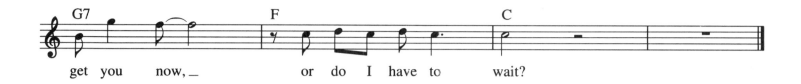

get you now, — or do I have to wait?

Ain't no use for me to work so hard,
I got two woman workin' in the rich folks yard.
Tell me how long do I have to wait?
Can I get you now, or do I have to hesitate?

I ain't your good man, neither you good man's son,
But I get in the place of your good man, till your
good man comes.
Tell me how long do I have to wait?
Can I get you now, or do I have to hesitate?

I ain't no miller, no miller's son,
But I can ground a little corn till your miller comes.
Tell me how long do I have to wait?
Can I get you now, or do I have to hesitate?

I ain't no grocery man, no grocery man's son,
But I can buy you a little groceries till your
grocery man comes.
Tell me how long do I have to wait?
Can I get you now, or do I have to hesitate?

I ain't no cradle-rocker, ain't no cradle-rocker's son,
But I can do a little rockin' for you, till the
cradle man comes.
Tell me how long do I have to wait?
Can I get you now, or do I have to hesitate?

I ain't no doctor, no doctor man's son,
But I can cure a few cases till the doctor man comes.
Tell me how long do I have to wait?
Can I get you now, or do I have to hesitate?

I ain't no bookkeeper, no bookkeeper's son,
I can keep a few books for you till your bookkeeper comes.
Tell me how long do I have to wait?
Can I get you now, or do I have to hesitate?

Well, I ain't no milkman, no milkman's son,
But I can keep you supplies, till your milkman comes.
Tell me how long do I have to wait?
Can I get you now, or do I have to hesitate?

I ain't no chauffeur, no chauffeur man's son,
But I can do a little drivin' till you chauffeur man comes.
Tell me how long do I have to wait?
Can I get you now, or do I have to hesitate?

I ain't got no woman, and I ain't got no kids,
I ain't got nobody's daughter to be bothered with.
Tell me how long do I have to wait?
Can I get you now, or do I have to hesitate?

I ain't been to heaven, but I've been told,
St. Peter taught the angels how to jelly roll.
Tell me how long do I have to wait?
Can I get you now, or do I have to hesitate?

I hitched up the mule and the mule wouldn't pull,
Took the harness off the mule, and put the harness on the bull.
Tell me how long do I have to wait?
Can I get you now, or do I have to hesitate?

The blacker the berry, the sweeter the juice,
I'd be a fool if I quit the woman I got 'cause it ain't no use.
Tell me how long do I have to wait?
Can I get you now, or do I have to hesitate?

I got hesitating stockings, hesitating shoes,
I got a hesitating woman singing me the hesitating blues.
Tell me how long do I have to wait?
Can I get you now, or do I have to hesitate?

If my good woman quits me, I ain't gonna wear no black,
I always got something to make her come runnin' back.
Tell me how long do I have to wait?
Can I get you now, or do I have to hesitate?

Men in the country hollering, "Whoa, ha, gee,"
Women in the city flyin' around cryin', "Who wants me?"
Tell me how long do I have to wait?
Can I get you now, or do I have to hesitate?

Ashes to ashes and dust to dust,
Just show me a woman a man can trust.
Tell me how long do I have to wait?
Can I get you now, or do I have to hesitate?

My mama told me when I was just six years old,
I gonna be a good woman got a son, God bless your soul.
Tell me how long do I have to wait?
Can I get you now, or do I have to hesitate?

I'm a King Bee

by James Moore

I'm a king bee, buzzin' all night long.(2X)
When you can hear me buzzin', there's some stinging goin' on.

I'm a king bee, I want you to be my queen.(2X)
When we get together, make honey the world ain't never seen.

I'm a king bee, buzzin' all night long.(2X)
I can make plenty honey, when your man is not at home.

Little Red Rooster

by Willie Dixon

Recorded by: Willie Dixon
Howlin' Wolf

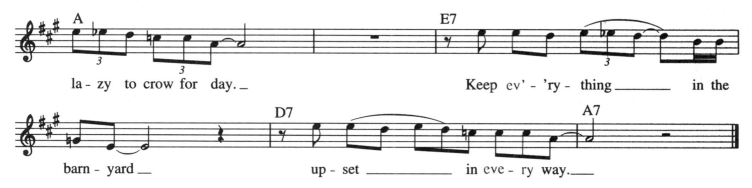

la - zy to crow for day. _ Keep ev' - 'ry - thing _____ in the

barn - yard _ up - set _____ in eve - ry way. _

The dogs begin to bark and the hounds begin to howl.(2X)
Oh, watch out strange kin people, the little red rooster is on the prowl.

If you see my little red rooster, please drive him home.(2X)
There's been no peace in the barnyard since my little red rooster's been gone.

Broken Hearted Blues

by Willie Dixon

Chills _ on my pil - low, _ ice - wa - ter in my ba - by's bed. _

Yeah, _ chills _ on my pil - low, ___ ice _ wa - ter in my ba - by's bed. _

— All the good things I have done for you wom - an,

and you left me for an - oth - er man. _

If you happen to see my baby, I want you to tell her I been cryin' on my knees.(2X)
Tell me pray to my master, please hope her back to me.

If I had ten million dollars, woman, you know I would give you every dime.(2X)
"... call me daddy one more time."

Shake Your Moneymaker

by Elmore James

Recorded by: Elmore James
Paul Butterfield

Love you, baby, tell you the reason why.(2X)
Every time you leave me, I want to lay down and die.

chorus

I got a baby, she lives up on the hill.(2X)
Says she gonna love me but I don't think she will.

chorus

I got a gal and she just won't be true.(2X)
She got to the place, won't do a thing I tell her to.

Back Door Man

by Willie Dixon

Recorded by: Howlin' Wolf

chorus

I____ am _____ a back door man._____

I__ am_____ a back door man._____ Well, the

men don't_ know but the little girls___ un-der-stand._

verse

When eve-ry-bod-y's tryin' to sleep, _ I'm some-where_ mak-in' my

mid-night creep._ Just the morn-in'_ the roost-er crow,____

some-thin' tell__ me__ I got to go.__

They take me to the doctor, shot full of holes,
Nurse cried, can't save his soul.
Accused him for murder, first degree,
Judge wife cried, let the man go free.

When everybody's tryin' to sleep,
I'm somewhere makin' my midnight creep,
Every morning the rooster crow,
Something tell me I got to go.

Cop's wife cried, "Don't kick him down,
Rather be dead, six feet in the ground."
When you come home you can eat pork and beans,
I eat more chicken any man seen.

Cool Drink of Water Blues

Recorded by: Tommy Johnson

I ask for water, and she gave me gas-o-line.

I ask for wa-ter, give me gas-o-line.

I ask for wa-ter and she

give me gas-o-line. Lord, Lord-y Lord.

Cryin', Lord, I wonder, will I ever get back home?
Cryin', Lord, I wonder, I ever get back home?
Lord, Lordy Lord.
I went to the depot, looked up on the board,
I asked the conductor how long has this Eastbound train been gone?

I asked the conductor could I ride the blinds?
Son, buy your ticket, buy your ticket, for that train ain't none of mine,
Son, buy your ticket, train ain't none of mine,
Son, buy your ticket, train ain't none of mine,
Lord, Lordy Lord.

Crosscut Saw

Recorded by: Albert King

I'm a cross-cut saw, baby, drag me 'cross your

log. You know I'm a cross-cut saw,

just drag me a-cross your log.___ I cut your

wood so eas - y for you, you can't help but say I saw.___

Some call me Woodchoppin' Sam, some call me Woodcuttin' Jim.(2X)
The last girl I cut wood for, wants me back again.

I got a double blade axe that really cuts good.(2X)
I'm a crosscut saw, just bury me in your wood.

Early in the Morning

Recorded by: Elmore James

Well, it's ear - ly in the morn - ing, _____ and my ba - by can't be found.

Well, it's ear - ly in the morn - ing _____ and my ba - by can't be

found. I'm gon - na pack up and leave her _____

___ if she don't stop run - nin' 'round.

Well, I got to leave my baby, 'cause she gives me such a thrill.(2X)
Well, she takes me back in the mornin', and I hope she will.

She can get so sentimental when the lights are way down low.(2X)
The way that gal can thrill me, make any man come back for more.

Rambling on My Mind
by Robert Johnson

Recorded by: Robert Johnson

I got ram-blin',__ I got ram-blin' on my mind.__

I got ram-blin',__ I got ram-blin' on my mind. Hate to

leave my ba-by, but she treats me so un-kind.__

I got mean things, I got mean things all on my mind.(2X)
Hate to leave you here, babe, but you treat me so unkind.

Runnin' down to the station, catch the first mail train I see.(2X)
I got the blues about miss so-and-so, and the child's got the blues about me.

I'm leaving this morning with my arms fold up and cryin'.(2X)
I hate to leave my baby, but she treats me so unkind.

Silver City Bound
Words and Music by Huddie Ledbetter
Edited with New Additional Material by Alan Lomax

Recorded by: Leadbelly

Freely *chorus*

Sil-ver Cit-y bound, I'm Sil-ver Cit-y bound,

Well, I tell my ba-by I'm Sil-ver Cit-y bound.

Hey,__ Blind Lem-on gon-na ride on down.

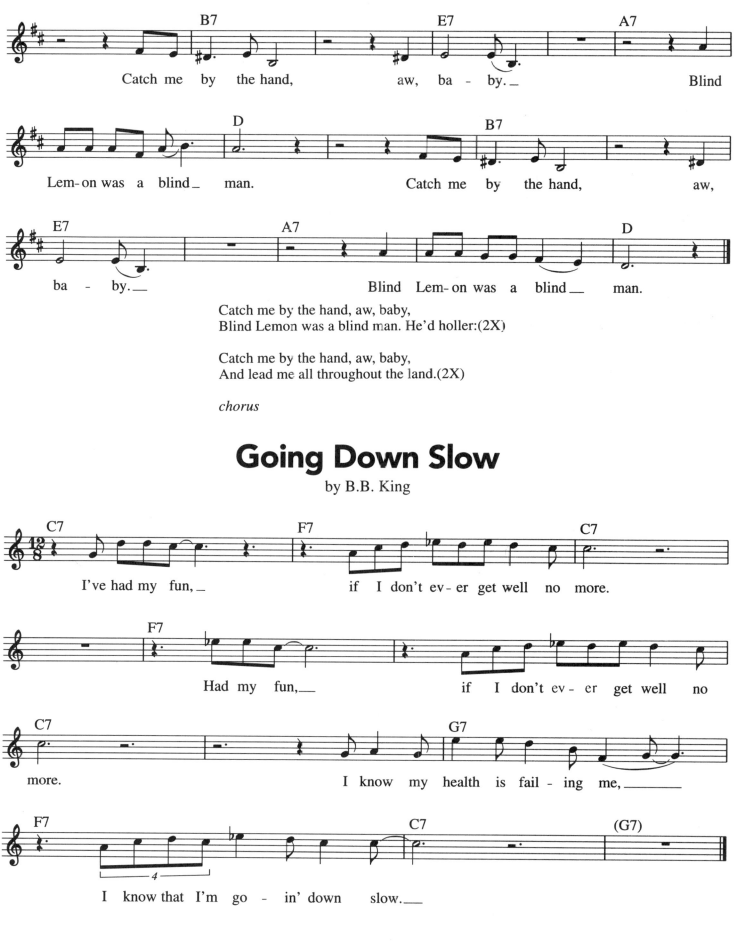

Catch me by the hand, aw, baby,
Blind Lemon was a blind man. He'd holler:(2X)

Catch me by the hand, aw, baby,
And lead me all throughout the land.(2X)

chorus

Going Down Slow

by B.B. King

Won't somebody write my mother, and tell her the shape I'm in?(2X)
I want you to tell her to pray for me, ask her to forgive me for my sins.

Mother, please don't send me no doctor, a doctor can't do me no good.(2X)
Back when I was a young boy, I just didn't do the things I should.

The First Time I Met the Blues

by E. Montgomery

Recorded by: Buddy Guy

The first time I met the blues,_____ I was walk - in' down__ through the woods._____

Yeah,_____ the first time I met__ the blues,__ don't you know__ I was walk - in' down through the woods._____

Yeah,_____ stop by my house__ to play the blues, blues, you know you done me all the harm__ that you could.

The blues got after me, they ride me from tree to tree.(2X)
Yeah, you should have heard me beggin', blues, blues, don't bother me.

Yeah, good morning blues, blues I wonder what you're doin' here so soon.(2X)
You know you'll be with me every morning, every night, and every noon.

Seventh Son

by Willie Dixon

Recorded by: Willie Dixon

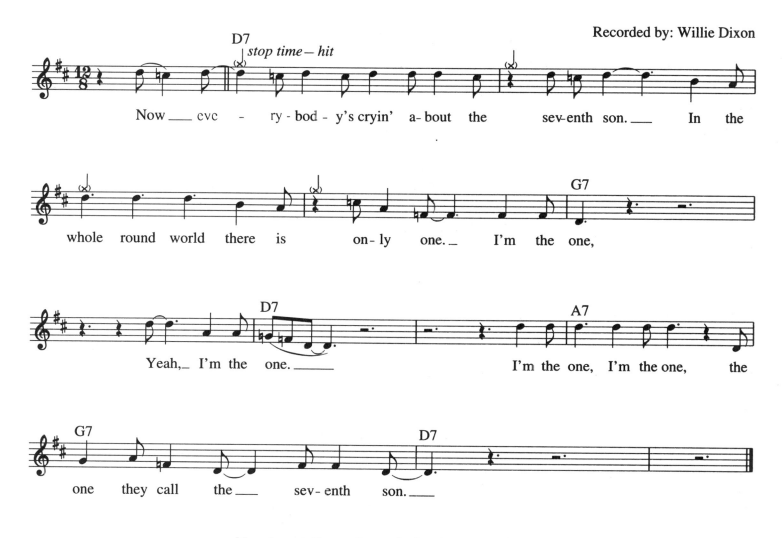

Now I can tell your future, before it comes to pass.
I can do things for you, make your heart feel glad.
I can look in the skies, and predict the rain.
I can tell when a woman's got another man.

I'm the one, I'm the one.
I'm the one, I'm the one,
I'm the one they call the seventh son.

I can hold you close and squeeze you tight.
I can make you grab for me, both day and night.
I can heal the sick, I can raise the dead.
I can make you little girl, talk you out of your head.

I'm the one, I'm the one.
I'm the one, I'm the one,
I'm the one they call the seventh son.

I can talk these words, and sound so sweet.
And make your lovin' heart even skip a beat.
I can take you, baby, hold you in my arms,
And make the flesh quiver, lovely forms.

Phone Booth

Written by Robert Cray, Dennis Walker. Michael Vannice and Richard Cousins

Recorded by: Robert Cray

Been walking all day, friends I can't find.
Heart's so cold, had to buy me some wine.
Calling you, baby, took my very last dime.

Said call Big Rita, anytime day or night.
You know, I'm broke and I'm cold, baby, and I hope you'll treat me right.
I'm in a phone booth baby with the cold right outside.

Rolling Stone

by Muddy Waters

Recorded by: Muddy Waters

I went my baby's house, and I sit down on her sill.
She said, "Come on in (Muddy), my mother's just not well."
Shaw' 'nuff, just not well,
Shaw' 'nuff, just not well.
Oh, Lord, oh, well.

Well my mother told my father just before I was born,
"I got a boy child comin',
Gonna be a rolling stone."(3X)
Oh, well, he's a...

Well, I feel, yes I feel, baby, like my lowdown time ain't long.
I'm gonna cut the twist train, Spokane bound.
Back down the road I'm goin', boy.(3X)
Shaw' 'nuff

Rev. Robert Wilkins and Skip James

My Babe

by Willie Dixon

Recorded by: Willie Dixon

My ba - by don't stand no cheat - in', my babe.

My ba - by don't stand no cheat - in', my babe.

My ba - by don't stand no cheat - in', she

don't stand none of that mid - night creep - in'. My babe,

true lit - tle ba - by, ____ my babe.

My babe, I know she love me, my babe.(2x)
Oh yeah, I know she love me.
She don't do nothing but kiss and hug me.
My babe, true little baby, my babe.

My babe, she don't stand no cheatin', my babe.(2x)
Oh no, she don't stand no cheatin'.
Everything she do she do so pleasin'.
My babe, true little baby, my babe.

My baby don't stand no fooling, my babe.(2X)
My baby don't stand no foolin'.
When she's hot there ain't no coolin'.
My babe, true little baby, my babe.

No More Lovers

by Arthur Big Boy Crudup

Recorded by: Arthur Crudup

We won't be no more lov - ers, we gon' be ___ old friends. ___

We won't be no more lov - ers, we gon - na be old friends. ___

You can help me find a wom - an, I'll help you out with your man. ___

I was in love withe you baby, you was in love with someone else. (2X)
You know darn well that I loved you, and wanted you for myself.

I even tried to love you when I knew you was untrue. (2X)
You went away and left me, I'll find someone who is true.

Reprinted by Permission of Crudup Music

Life is Like That

Words and Music by Memphis Slim
Edited with new material by Alan Lomax

Recorded by: Memphis Slim

verse

You've got to cry a lit - tle, ___ die a lit - tle,

chorus

Well, and some - times you got to lie a lit - tle. ___ Oh, life is like that, ___

well that's ___ what you've got ___ to do. ___ Well, if you

don't un - der - stand,__ peo - ple, I'm __ sor - ry for you.

Sometimes you'll be held up, sometimes held down,
Well, sometimes your best friends don't even want you around, you know...

chorus

There's some things you got to keep, some things you got to repeat,
People, happiness is never complete, you know...

chorus

Sometimes you'll be helpless, sometime you'll be restless,
Well, keep on strugglin' so long as your not breathless...

Mean Old Bed Bug Blues

Recorded by: Bessie Smith

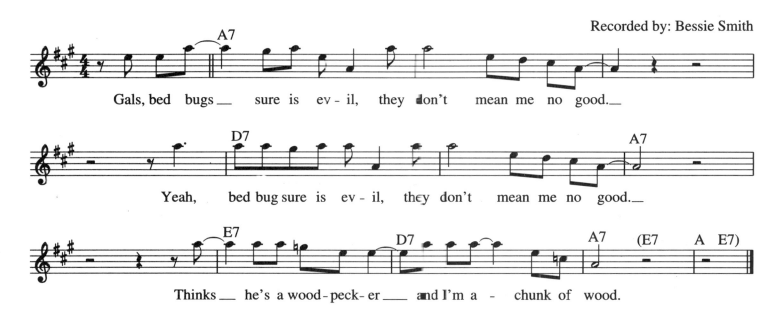

Gals, bed bugs __ sure is ev - il, they don't mean me no good.__

Yeah, bed bug sure is ev - il, they don't mean me no good.__

Thinks __ he's a wood-peck-er __ and I'm a - chunk of wood.

When I lay down at night, I wonder how can a poor gal sleep.(2X)
When some is holding my hand, others eating my feet.

Bed bug as big as a jackass, will bite you and stand and grin.(2X)
Will drink all the bed but for them turn around and bite you again.

Something moan in the corner, I went over and see.(2X)
It was the bed bug a prayin', Lord, gimme some more cheese.

Born in Chicago

by Nick Gravenites

Recorded by: Paul Butterfield

I was born in Chi-ca-go in nine-teen __ and for-ty one. __

I was born in Chi-ca-go in nine-teen __ and for-ty one. __

__ Well, my Fa-ther told __ me

"Son, you had bet-ter get a gun." __

bass vamp figure

My first friend went down when I was seventeen years old.(2X)
Well, there's one thing I can say about that boy, he's got soul.

Well, my second friend went down when I was twenty-one years of age.(2X)
There is one thing I can say about that boy, he's got soul.

Well, now rules are alright if there is someone left to play the game.(2X)
All my friends are going, and things just don't seem the same.

Blues on the Ceiling

Words and Music by Fred Neil

Recorded by: Fred Neil

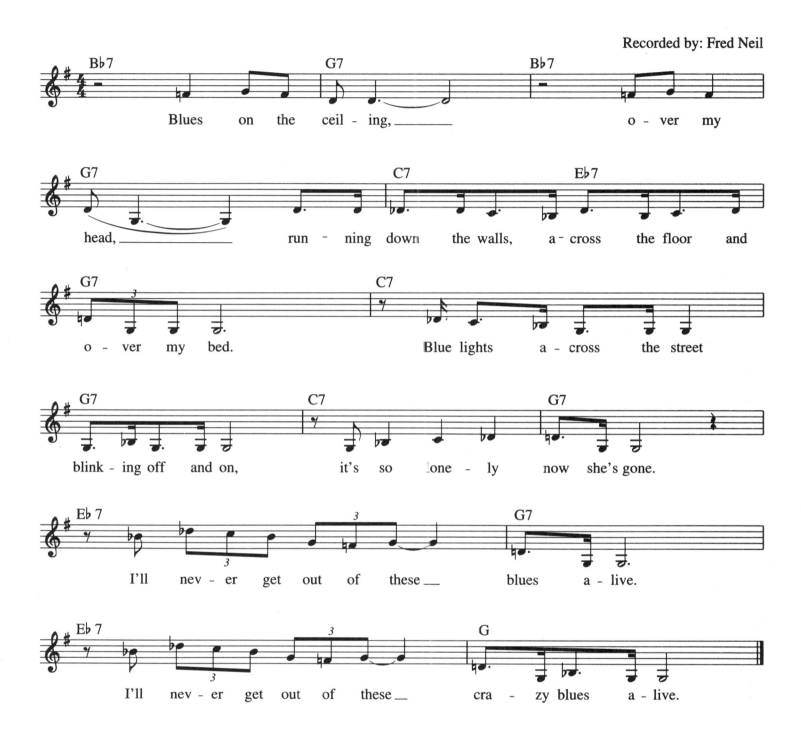

Love had been a dirty five-letter word to me,
I was into the blues over my head.
Blue was all I could see, up to my neck in misery.
I'll never get out of these blues alive.
I'll never get out of these crazy blues alive.

Blues keep on fooling with my weary head,
Cocaine couldn't numb the pain. I'd be better off dead.
The lights gone out, at last I sleep.
I'll never get out of these blues alive.
I'll never get out of these crazy blues alive.

You Gonna Quit Me Baby

Recorded by: Arthur "Blind" Blake

You gon - na quit me, ba - by, good as I been to you.___ Good as I been to you, Lord, Lord, ___ Good as I been ___ to ___ you.

Give you my money, honey, buy your shoes and clothes, Lord, Lord.
Buy your shoes and clothes, Lord, Lord,
Buy your shoes and clothes.

You're gonna quit me baby, put me out of doors.
Put me out of doors, Lord, Lord,
Put me out of doors.

Six months on the chain gang, b'lieve me ain't no fun.
B'lieve me, ain't no fun, Lord, Lord,
B'lieve me, ain't no fun.

Jailhouse ain't no plaything, b'lieve me, 'tain't no lie.
B'lieve me, 'taint no lie, Lord, Lord,
B'lieve me, 'tain't no lie.

Day you quit me, baby, that's the day you die, Lord, Lord.
That's the day you die, Lord, Lord,
That's the day you die.

Jim Crow

Words and Music by Huddie Ledbetter

Recorded by: Leadbelly

Bunk John - son told me too, these old Jim Crow - is - ms ___ dead bad luck for me and you. I been

trav - lin',   I been   trav-lin' from shore to _____ shore.   Ev-'ry -

where I have been,_   I   find   some old ___ Jim   Crow.

One thing, people, I want everybody to know,
You gonna find some Jim Crow every place you go.

Down in Louisiana, Tennessee, Georgia's a mighty good place to go,
And get together, break up this old Jim Crow.

I want to tell you people something that you don't know,
It's alotta Jim Crow in the moving picture show.

I'm gonna sing this verse, I ain't gonna sing no more,
Please get together, break up this old Jim Crow.

The Blues Never Die

Ev'- ry-bod-y won- drin'_   where_ the blues_ come from. _

Ev' - 'ry-bod-y won- drin'_   where _____ did the blues come from._

—   Way_ back in the low lands, __

right   off ___ of my coun-try farm. ___

When you in trouble, blues is a man's best friend.(2X)
Blues ain't gonna ask you where you goin', and the blues ain't gonna ask you where you been.

We can't let the blues die, blues don't mean no harm.(2X)
I'm gonna move back in the lowlands, that's where the blues come from.

Worrying You Off My Mind

Recorded by: Big Bill Broonzy

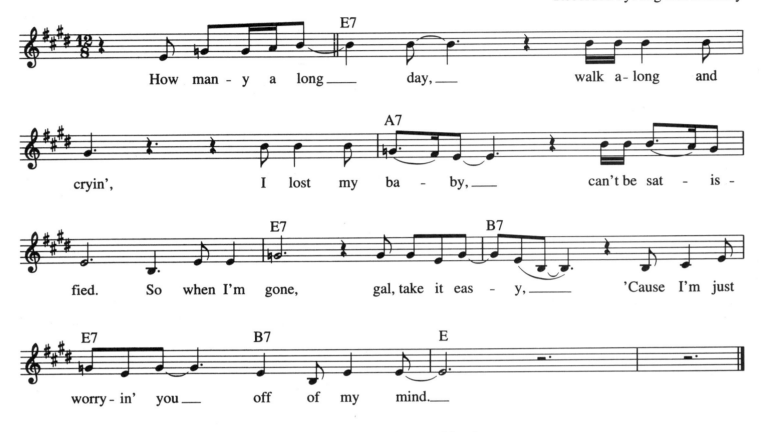

How man - y a long ____ day, ___ walk a- long and cryin', I lost my ba - by, ___ can't be sat - is - fied. So when I'm gone, gal, take it eas - y, ___ 'Cause I'm just worry - in' you __ off of my mind. __

When you get in trouble, haven't got a friend,
Just take it easy, they'll need your help again.
So when I'm gone, gal, take it easy,
'Cause I'm just worrying you off of my mind.

Now, ain't it hard to live alone,
Just (as) hard to be married and break up your home.
So when I'm gone, gal, take it easy,
'Cause I'm just worrying you off of my mind.

But that's alright, that's alright for you,
You need me some mornin', when I won't need you.
So when I'm gone, gal, take it easy,
'Cause I'm just worrying you off of my mind.

When I was down, lost my wife and my friend,
When I got my money, they all come back again.
So when I'm gone, gal take it easy,
'Cause I'm just worrying you off of my mind.

Money and pretty women run hand in hand,
When they raisin' a squabble, takin' some woman's man.
So when I'm gone, gal, take it easy,
'Cause I'm just worrying you off of my mind.

De Kalb Blues

Words and Music by Huddie Ledbetter
Edited with new additional material by John A. Lomax and Alan Lomax

Recorded by: Leadbelly

De Kalb blues,_ babe, make me feel _ so bad. _

De Kalb blues,_ babe, make me feel _____ so bad. _

Just to think _ a - bout _ the times _ I once have had. _

Wasn't for the powder and the straightnin' comb.(2x)
Lord, these De Kalb women would not have no home.

Buy me a pistol, get me a Gatlin' gun.(2X)
Ever catch you, baby, we gonna have some fun.

Some folks told me De Kalb blues ain't bad.(2X)
It's the worry'st blues that I ever had.

If the blues was whiskey, I'd stay drunk all the time.(2X)
Stay drunk,baby, to get you off of my mind.

Feelin', baby, jump overboard and drown.(2X)
Singin' 'bout my woman, she done left this town.

Jumped into the river and I started to drown.(2X)
Thought about my baby and I turned around.

Look here, baby, what more can I do?(2X)
Well, I had five dollars and I gave you two.

Dust Pneumonia Blues

Words and Music by Woody Guthrie

Recorded by: Woody Guthrie

C
I got that dust pneu - mo - ny, ___ pneu - mo - ny in my lung. ___

F
_ I got the dust pneu - mo - ny, ___ pneu - mo - ny in my lung. ___

C

G7
And I'm gon - na sing this dust pneu - mo - ny song. **C**

Now there ought to be some yodeling in this song.(2X)
But I can't yodel for the rattling in my lung.

My good gal sings the dust pneumony blues.(2X)
She loves me 'cause she's got the dust pneumony, too.

If it wasn't for choppin', my hoe would turn to rust.(2X)
I can't find a woman in this black old Texas dust.

Down in Oklahoma the wind blows mighty strong.(2X)
If you want to get a mama, just sing a California song.

Down in Texas my gal fainted in the rain.(2X)
I threw a bucket of dirt in her face just to bring her back again.

New York Town

Words and Music by Woody Guthrie

Recorded by: Woody Guthrie

C **C7**
I was stand-ing down in New York town one day. ___

F **C**
Stand - ing down in New York town one day.

G7 **C**
I was stand - ing down in New York town one day.

Sing - ing, hey, hey, hey, hey. ____

I was broke, I didn't have a dime.(3X)
Every good man gets a little hard luck sometime.

Down and out and he ain't got a dime.(3X)
I'm gonna ride that new morning railroad train.

Holdin' my last dollar in my hand.(3X)
Looking for a woman that's looking for a man.

If you don't want me, you don't have to stall.(3X)
I can get more woman than a passenger train can haul.

If you don't want me, just please leave me be.(3X)
I can buy more lovers than the Civil War set free.

Crossroads Blues

by Robert Johnson

Recorded by: Robert Johnson

I went to the cross - roads, fell down on my knees. ____

I went to the cross - roads, ____ fell down on my knees.

I asked the Lord _ a - bove, have mer - cy, ____

save poor Bob if you please. ____

Standin' at the crossroad, tried to flag a ride.(2X)
Didn't nobody seem to know me, everybody pass me by.

Standin' at the crossroad, risin' sun goin' down.(2X)
I believe to my souls, po' Bob is sinkin' down.

You can run, you can run, tell my friend Willie Brown.(2X)
That I got the crossroad blues this mornin', Lord, I'm sinkin' down.

And I went to the crossroad, mama, I looked east and west.(2X)
Lord, I didn't have no sweet woman, oh well, babe, in my distress.

My Handy Man Ain't Handy No More

Recorded by: Bessie Smith

2. Time after time, if I'm not right there at his heels,
He lets that poor horse in my stable miss his meals.
There's got to be some changes 'cause each day reveals,
My handy man ain't handy no more.

He used to turn in early and get up at dawn,
And full of new ambitions, he would trim the lawn.
Now, when he isn't sleeping all he does is yawn,
My handy man ain't handy no more

bridge
Once he used to have so much endurance.
Now, it looks like he needs life insurance.

I used to brag about my handy man's technique,
Around the house he was a perfect indoor sheik.
But now the spirit's willing but the flesh is weak.
My handy man ain't handy no more.

Mind Your Own Business

by Hank Williams

Recorded by: Hank Williams

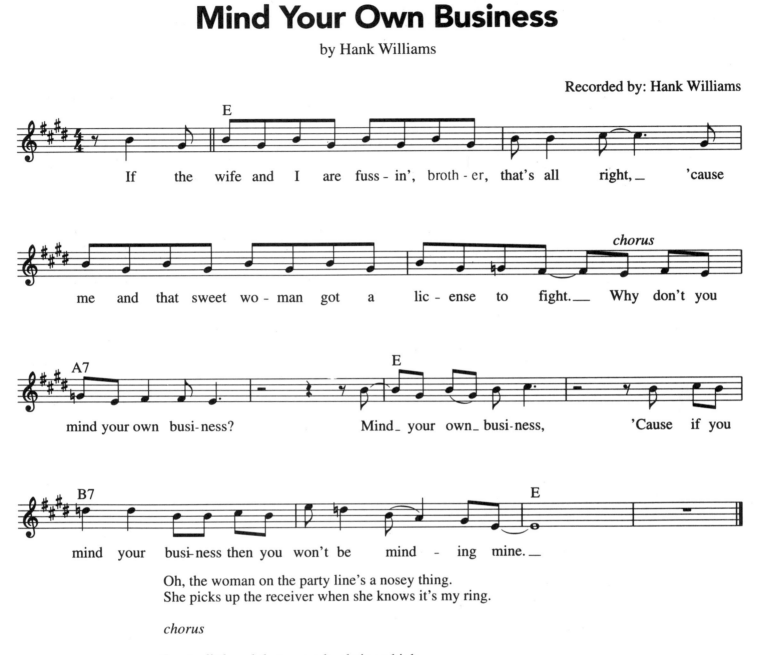

Oh, the woman on the party line's a nosey thing.
She picks up the receiver when she knows it's my ring.

chorus

I got a little gal that wears her hair up high.
The boys all whistle when she walks by.

chorus

Well, if I want to honky tonk around till two or three.
Now brother, that's my headache, don't you worry 'bout me.

chorus

Minding other people's business seems to be high toned.
I got all that I can do just to mind my own.

chorus

The World Has Gone Wrong

Recorded by: Mississippi Sheiks

Strange things have hap-pened, that nev-er be-fore, My ba-by told me

I would have to go. I can't be good no more, once like I did be-fore.

I can't be good, ba-by, hon-ey be-cause the world's going wrong.

In bed this morning, ain't got no home,
No use a worryin', 'cause the world's gone wrong.

chorus

I told you baby, right to your head,
If I didn't leave you, I'd have to kill you dead.

chorus

I tried to be lovin', and treat you kind,
But it seems like now, I've got no love in mind.

chorus

If you have a woman, and she don't be kind,
Pray to the good Lord to get her off your mind.

chorus

Then when you been good now, can't do no more,
Just tell her kindly, there is a front door.

chorus

Pack up my suitcase, pass me my hat,
No use to ask me, baby, 'cause I'll never be back.

chorus

Blues and Booze

Recorded by: Ma Rainey

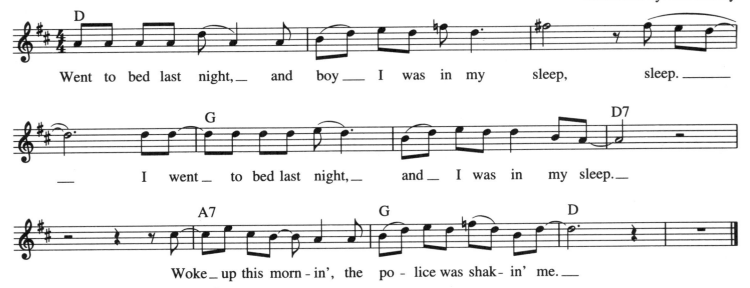

I went to the jailhouse, drunk and blue as I could be.(2X)
But that cruel old judge sent my man away from me.

They carried me to the courthouse, Lordy, how I was cryin'.(2X)
They jailed me sixty days in jail, and money couldn't pay my fine.

Sixty days ain't long if you can spend them as you choose.(2X)
But this seems like jail than a cell where there ain't no booze.

My life is all a misery when I cannot get my booze.(2X)
I spend every dime on liquor, got to have the booze to go with these blues.

Crazy Man Blues

Recorded by: Saunders "Sonny" Terry

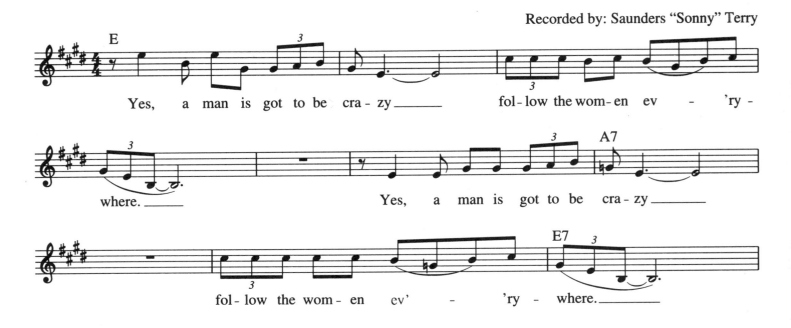

Well, I ain't sing-in' this song 'cause I ain't got no one,____

____ Yes, you know I can set some-bod-y, pal.

Yes, a man's got to be crazy to think he got a woman all by himself.(2X)
I say as I'm back in town,
Yes, you know she's cutting out with somebody else.

Yes, a man is crazy to give one woman all his pay.(2X)
I said, before I'd be like them,
I'd walk out of the front door to stay.

Mystery Train

Recorded by: Paul Butterfield

Train I ride,____ is six-teen_ coach-es long.____

Train I ride____ is six-teen_ coach-es long.____

Well, that long_ black train,____ take my ba-by and gone.____

rhythmic feel

Mystery train, rolling down the track.(2X)
Well, it took my baby and it won't be coming back.

Train, train, rolling 'round the bend.(2X)
Well, it took my baby, won't be back again.

Train I ride, sixteen coaches long.(2X)
Well, that long black train take my baby and gone.

Hey, Bo Diddley

by Ellas McDaniel

Recorded by: Bo Diddley

Knocked and knocked till her fist got sore. Hey, Bo Did - dley. ___

When she turned and walked a - way, Hey, Bo Did - dley. ___

All you could hear my ba - by say: Hey, Bo Did - dley, ___

chorus

Hey, Bo Did - dle - y, ___ Hey, Bo Did - dle - y, ___

Hey, Bo Did - dle - y, ___ Hey, Bo - Did - dle - y. ___

E vamp figure

Saw my baby run across the field.
Slippin' and slidin' in that automobile.
Hollered at my baby then towed her away.
Slipped off from me like a Cadillac Eight.

Why Should I Be Blue

Recorded by: Walter Davis

Why____ should I be wor-ried,___ and why should I be

so blue?___ Why should I be____

wor-ried, why __ should I be so blue? Lord, it's all__

__ on ac-count of, all on ac-count of you.___

How can I sleep and keep from worryin', how can I laugh and keep from cryin'?
Lord, every time I turn my back, you always doing something to change my mind.

I just flutters when I see you, like a little bird up in his nest.
Lord, sometime I think I love you, sometime I think I love my other little gal to death.

I can't keep from worryin', and I just can't keep from tellin' you lies.
Lord, I would do alright with you, baby, but you know you tried to be too wise.

You're Gonna Miss Me

by B.B King

Recorded by: B.B. King

Let me tell you peo-ple a low down thing or two.
I just can't stand that old e-vil way she do. You're gon-na
miss me, _____ you're gon-na miss me. _____ You're gon-na
miss me, ba-by, when I'm dead and gone. ___

I came home this morning, she wouldn't let me in.
She said, "Go away, baby, I've got too many friends."
You're gonna miss me, you're gonna miss me.
You're gonna miss me, baby, when I'm dead and gone.

It's hard to love a woman when the woman don't love you.
She'll treat you so low down and dirty, till you don't know what to do.
You're gonna miss me, you're gonna miss me.
You're gonna miss me, baby, when I'm dead and gone.

Bye bye, baby, I hope we meet again.
You won't be so evil, and you won't have so many friends.
You're gonna miss me, you're gonna miss me.
You're gonna miss me, baby, when I'm dead and gone.

Troubles, Troubles, Troubles

Recorded B.B. King

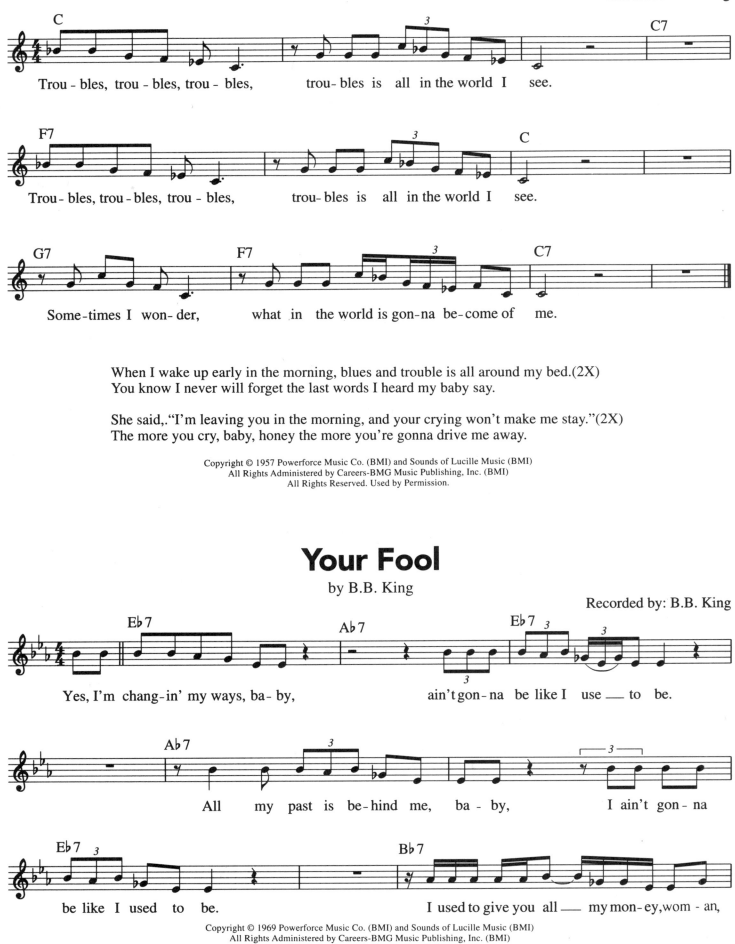

Trou-bles, trou-bles, trou-bles, trou-bles is all in the world I see.

Trou-bles, trou-bles, trou-bles, trou-bles is all in the world I see.

Some-times I won-der, what in the world is gon-na be-come of me.

When I wake up early in the morning, blues and trouble is all around my bed.(2X)
You know I never will forget the last words I heard my baby say.

She said,."I'm leaving you in the morning, and your crying won't make me stay."(2X)
The more you cry, baby, honey the more you're gonna drive me away.

Your Fool

by B.B. King

Recorded by: B.B. King

Yes, I'm chang-in' my ways, ba-by, ain't gon-na be like I use — to be.

All my past is be-hind me, ba-by, I ain't gon-na

be like I used to be. I used to give you all — my mon-ey, wom-an,

and I would-n't save a dime _____ for me.

Yeah, you used to treat me like a fool,
Still I loved everything you done
I was just your fool, I was your fool, baby,
Yes, if you ever, if you ever love me, woman,
Yes, I tell you, baby.

I Be's Troubled

Written by Muddy Waters

Recorded by: Muddy Waters

Well, I feel _____ to-mor-row like I feel to-day.

In' goin' pack my suit-case and make my get-a-way, Lord, I'm trou-bled, I'm

all wor-ried now. And I

nev-er been sat-is-fied,__ and I just can't keep from cry-in'.

Yeah, know somebody, some been talkin' to you.
I don't need no tellin', girl, I can watch the way you do.
Lord, I'm troubled, and I'm all worried now.
Yeah, I never been satisfied, and I just can't keep from cryin'.

Now goodbye, babe, got no more to say.
Just like I been tellin' you, girl, you gonna have to leave my bed.
Lord, I'm troubled, and I'm all worried now.
Yeah, I never been satisfied, and I just can't keep from cryin'.

Mama Let Me Lay it on You

Written by Mance Lipscomb

Recorded by: Walter Coleman

Ma-ma let me lay it on you, Ma-ma let me lay it on you.___ I

did ev'-ry-thing_ in this whole round world.___ Ma-ma let me lay it on you.___

Then I'm goin' upstairs, turn your lamp down low,
And if you bed breaks down,
Then you pile it on the floor.

I'm gonna buy you a diamond ring, baby, till you take that thing.
I did everything in this whole round world.
Mama let me lay it on you.

Mama let me lay it on you, mama let me lay it on you.
Did everything in this whole round world.
Baby, let me lay it on you.

Mama, pull off your dress, and put on your nightgown.
I got a funny feeling baby, in my back,.
Mama, won't you pile it down.

Salty Dog

by Mississippi John Hurt

Recorded by: Papa Charlie Jackson

chorus

Why don't you let me be_ your salt-y dog,_ don't want to be your

man at all.___ Salt-y dog,_ ma-ma's lit-tle salt-y dog.___

verse

Just like hun-tin' for a nee-dle in a bale of sand,_ tryn' to find a wom-an has-n't

got no man._ Salt-y dog,_ you salt-y dog._ Why don't you

let me be your salt - y dog. ___ Don't want to be your man at all. ___

Salt - y dog, ___ ma - ma's lit - tle salt - y dog. ___

Little fish, big fish, swimming in the water.
Come on back here, man, and give me my quarter
Salty dog, you salty dog.

chorus

God made the women and he made her mighty funny.
Kiss 'em on the mouth, just as sweet as any honey.
Salty dog, you salty dog.

chorus

Evil
Is Goin' On

Recorded by: Willie Dixon

If ___ you're a long way from home, ___ can't ___ sleep at night,

Grab ___ your tel - e - phone, ___ some - thin' just ain't right: ___ That's e - vil, ___

e - vil ___ is go - in' on. ___ I am

warn - ing you broth - er, you bet - ter watch your hap - py home. ___

Well, if you call her on the telephone,
And she answers awful slow,
Grab the first thing smokin',
If you have to hobo:

chorus

If you make it to your house,
knock on the front door,
Run around to the back,
You catch him just before he goes:

chorus

Green River Blues

Recorded by: Charlie Patton

I think I heard the Marion whistle blow.(2X)
And it blew just like my baby gettin' on board.

I'm goin' where the Southern cross the dog.(3X)

Some people say the Green River blues ain't bad.(2X)
Then it must not have been them Green River blues I had.

It was late last night, everything was still.(2X)
I could see my baby up on a lonesome hill.

How long, evening train been gone.(2X)
Yes, I'm worried now but I won't be worried long.

I'm goin' away, I know it may get lonesome here.(3X)

Don't Sell it, Don't Give it Away

Recorded by: Oscar Woods

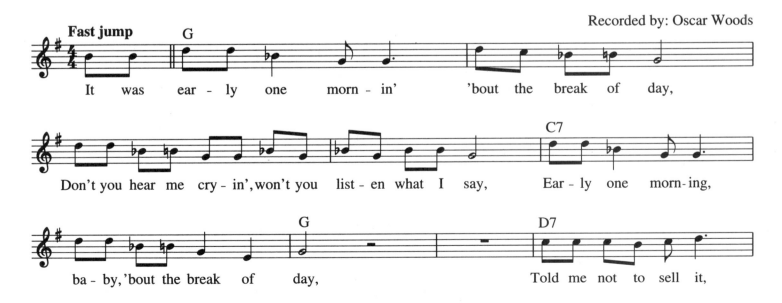

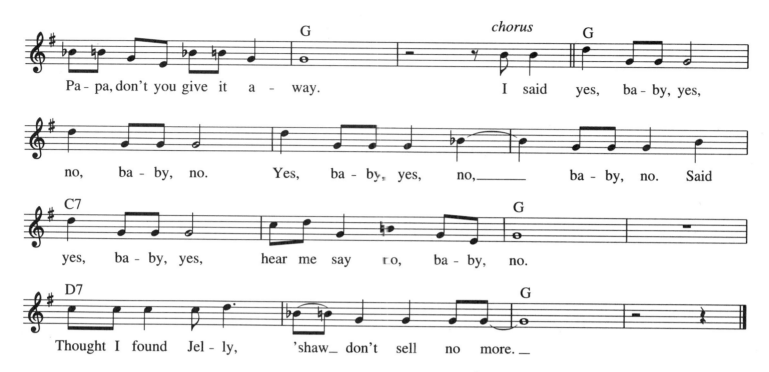

Pa - pa, don't you give it a - way. I said yes, ba - by, yes,
no, ba - by, no. Yes, ba - by, yes, no,_____ ba - by, no. Said
yes, ba - by, yes, hear me say no, ba - by, no.
Thought I found Jel - ly, 'shaw_ don't sell no more. _

You know you didn't want me, why did you call, don't you hear me cryin' little all and all,
You know you didn't want me, baby why did you call?
I can get more women than a passenger train can haul.

chorus

Texas Blues

Recorded by: Papa Charlie Jackson

I'm Tex - as bound,_ freight train on_ my mind. _ I'm
Tex - as bound, I got a freight train on_ my mind. _ If you miss_
_ me on the lo - cal look for me _ on _ the blind. _

My suitcase is packed, my trunk's already on.(2X)
You know by that, this sweet papa's going to be gone.

Just look around the corner, see that passenger train.(2X)
Be a long, long time before you see my face again.

It takes a good ol' fireman, a cool kind of engineer.(2X)
That'll pull that train, take me away from here.

I'm Texas bound, got no time to lose.(2X)
'Cause my sweet mama quit me, left me with the Texas blues.

Catfish Blues

by Muddy Waters

Fast jump feel

Recorded by: Robert Petway

Well, if I were a catfish, mama, swimmin' deep down in the deep blue sea,
Have these gals now, sweet mama, sittin' out,
Sittin' out doors for me,
Sittin' out doors for me,
Sittin' out doors for me,
Sittin' out doors for me,
Sittin' out doors for me.

Well, I went down to the church house, they called on me to pray,
Got on my knees now, mama, I didn't know not, not a word to say,
Not a word to say,
Not a word to say,
Not a word to say,
Not a word to say,
Not a word to say.

I'm gonna write, write me a letter baby, I'm gonna write it just to see,
See if my baby, my baby, do she thinkin' of, little ol' think of me,
Little ol' think of me,
Little ol' think of me,
Little ol' think of me,
Little ol' think of me,
Little ol' think of me.

I Crave My Pigmeat

Recorded by: Blind Boy Fuller

Now, pig - meat is tak - en to - day, to - day, ___ some-thing I do crave. Now, pig - meat is tak - en to - day, to - day, ___ some-thing I do crave. ___ Ash to ash - es and dust to dust, ___ Show me a wom - an that a man can trust. Pig - meat tak - en to - day, to - day, ___ some-thing I do crave,_ I mean it. Some - thing I do crave._

'Now, pigmeat is kicking today, today, something I do crave.(2X)
Had a little gal, she was little and low,
She used to shake it but she won't no more.
Now pigmeat is kicking today, today, something I do crave, I mean it.
Something I do crave.

Now, pigmeat is kicking today, today, something I do crave.(2X)
Looked down the road as far as I could see,
The boy's had my woman and the blues had me.
Now pigmeat is kicking today, today, something I do crave,I mean it.
Something I do crave.

Now, pigmeat is kicking today, today, something I do crave.(2X)
Ashes to ashes and sand to sand,
Show me a woman ain't got a back door man.
Now pigmeat is kicking today, today, something I do crave, I mean it.
Something I do crave.

From Four Until Late

by Robert Johnson

Recorded by: Robert Johnson

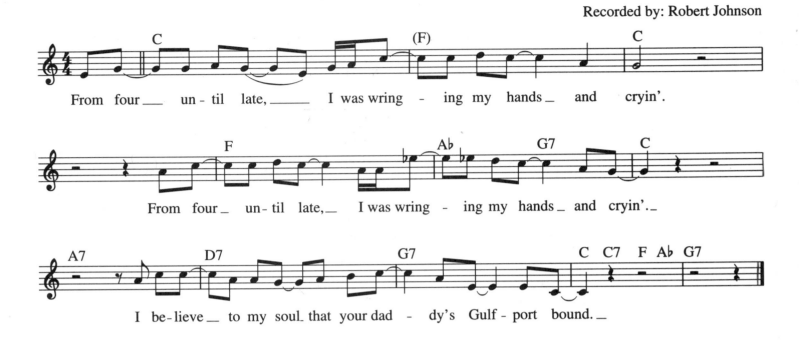

From four __ un - til late, ____ I was wring - ing my hands __ and cryin'.

From four __ un - til late, __ I was wring - ing my hands __ and cryin'. __

I be-lieve __ to my soul __ that your dad - dy's Gulf - port bound. __

From Memphis to Norfolk is a thirty-six hours' ride.(2X)
A man is like a prisoner, and he's never satisfied.

A woman is like a dresser, some man always ramblin' through its drawers.(2X)
It 'cause so many men, wear an apron over-all.

From four until late, she get with a no good bunch and clown.(2X)
Now she won't do nothin', but tear a good man's reputation down.

When I leave this town, I'm gon' bid you fare, farewell.(2X)
And when I return again, you'll have a great long story to tell.

Used by Permission of King of Spades Music

Three Hours Past Midnight

by Johnny Watson and Sam Ling

Recorded by: Johnny "Guitar" Watson

Here it is _____ three hours __ past mid-night, and my ba - by's __ no-

where _ a-round. Well, here it is _____ three hours past mid-night,

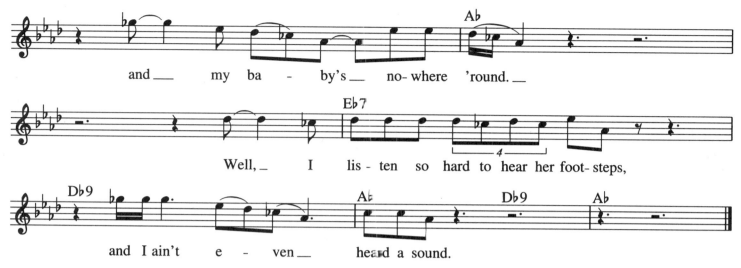

and __ my ba - by's __ no- where 'round. __

Well, _ I lis - ten so hard to hear her foot- steps,

and I ain't e - ven __ heard a sound.

Yes, I tossed and tumbled on my pillow, but I just can't close eyes. (2X)
If my baby don't come back pretty quick, yes I just can't
satisfied.

Well, I want my baby, I want her by my side. (2X)
Well, if she don't come home pretty soon, yes I just can't
be satisfied.

When My Heart Beats Like a Hammer

Recorded by: B.B. King

When my heart gets to beat- in' like a ham - mer, _____ and my eyes get full of

tears. When my heart gets to beat- in' like a ham - mer, _____

__ and my eyes get full of tears. You on - ly been

gone twen- ty- four hours, _____ but it seems like a mil - lion years.

If I ever mistreat you darlin', God knows I never meant no harm.(2X)
You know I'm just a little country boy, that was raised down on the farm.

You give me so much trouble, I don't know what to do.(2X)
I ain't got nothing now, and it's all on account of you.

Roberta

Words and Music by Huddie Ledbetter
Edited with New Additional Material by John A. Lomax and Alan Lomax

Recorded by: Leadbelly

Run here, Ro - ber - ta, _____ sit down on my knee. _

Run here, Ro - ber - ta, sit down on my knee. _

Got some-thing to tell you, and that's been wor - ryin' me. _____

I went down to the river, I sat down on the ground.(2X)
I'm gonna stay right here, Lord, till Roberta comes down.

Oh, Roberta, tell me how long, how long?(2X)
I'm gonna wait for you baby, I've gotta see you since you been gone.

Well, way up the river, just as far as I could see.(2X)
Lord, I thought I'd find my old time used to be.

She was a brownskin woman, she had black wavy hair.(2X)
And I can't subscribe her, anymore, anywhere.

I'm going to the station and talk to the chief of police.(2X)
Roberta done quit me, I can't see no peace.

Kindhearted Woman Blues

by Robert Johnson

Recorded by: Robert Johnson

I got a kind - heart - ed wom - an, _____

do an - y - thing _____ in this world for me. _

I got a kind - heart - ed wom - an,

do an-y-thing in this world for me. ____

But these e - vil-heart - ed wom-an,

man, they will not let me be. ____

I love my baby, my baby don't love me.(2X)
But I really love that woman, can't stand to let her be.

Ain't but one thing, make Mr. Johnson drink,
I's worried 'bout how you treat me, baby, I begin to think.
Oh, babe, my life don't feel the same,
You break my heart, when you call Mr. So and So's name.

She's a kindhearted woman, she studies evil all the time.(2X)
You well's to kill me, as to have it on your mind.

Goodbye Baby

by Sam Ling, Joe Josea and Jules Taub

Recorded by: Elmore James

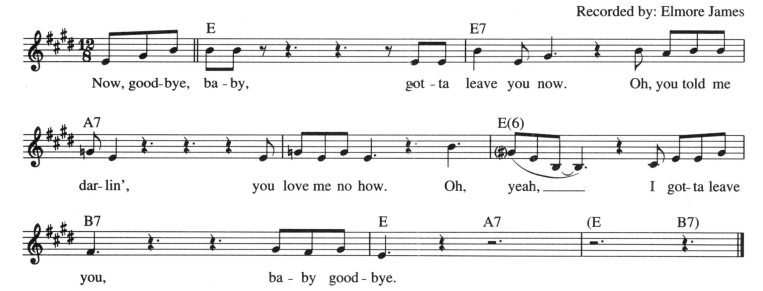

Now, good-bye, ba-by, got - ta leave you now. Oh, you told me

dar-lin', you love me no how. Oh, yeah, ____ I got-ta leave

you, ba - by good - bye.

Aw baby, here's my right hand
I love you, baby, I can't get you to understand.
Oh, bye, goodbye, baby, baby goodbye.

Aw yes, here's all of me.
I'll take you, baby, to some place you oght to be.
Oh, bye now, goodbye, baby goodbye.

Muddy Waters

Hellhound on My Trail

by Robert Johnson

Recorded by: Robert Johnson

If today was Christmas eve, if today was Christmas eve,
And tomorrow was Christmas day.
If today was Christmas eve and tomorrow was Christmas day.
All I would need is my little sweet rider,
Just to pass the time away, to pass the time away.

You sprinkled hot foot powder, mmm, around my door,
All around my door.
You sprinkled hot foot powder, all around your daddy's door.
It keeps me with ramblin' mind rider,
Every old place I go, every old place I go.

I can tell the wind is risin', the leaves tremblin' on the tree,
Tremblin' on the tree.
I can tell the wind is risin', leaves tremblin' on the tree.
All I need is my little sweet woman.
And to keep my company, hey, hey, hey, hey, my company.

Used by Permission of King o' Spades Music

Come on in My Kitchen

by Robert Johnson

Recorded by: Robert Johnson

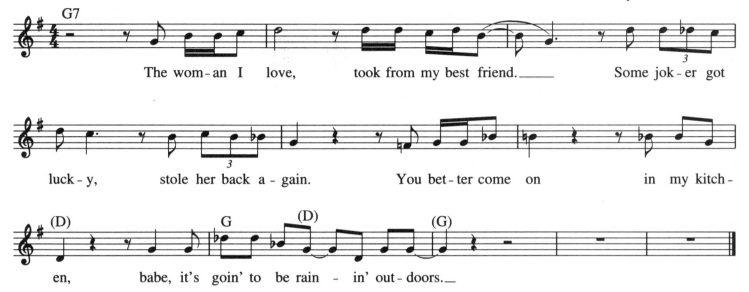

The wom-an I love, took from my best friend.____ Some jok-er got

luck-y, stole her back a-gain. You bet-ter come on in my kitch-

en, babe, it's goin' to be rain-in' out-doors.__

Oh, she's gone, I know she won't come back.
I've taken the last nickel out of her nation sack.
You better come on in my kitchen, baby, it's goin' to be rainin' outdoors.

(*Spoken:* Oh, can't you hear that wind howl?)
Can't you hear that wind howl?
You better come on in my kitchen, baby, it's goin' to be rainin' outdoors.

When a woman gets in trouble, everybody throws her down.
Lookin' for her good friend, none can't be found.
You better come on in my kitchen, baby, it's goin' to be rainin' outdoors.

Winter time's comin', it's goin' to be slow.
You can make the winter, babe, that's dry long so.
You better come on in my kitchen, 'cause it's goin' to be rainin' outdoors.

It Makes My Love Come Down

by Bessie Smith

When I see two sweet-hearts spoon,__ un-der-neath the

Wild about my toodle-oh,
When I gets my toodle-oh.
It makes my love come down, want every pound.
Hear me cryin', it makes my love come down.

Likes my coffee, likes my tea,
Daffy about my stingeree.
It makes my love come down, I wanna be around.
Oh, sweet papa, it makes my love come down.

If you want to hear me rave,
Honey, give me what I crave.
It makes my love come down, actin' like a clown.
Can't help from braggin, it makes my love come down.

Come on and be my desert sheik, you're so strong and I'm so weak.
It makes my love come down, to be love-land bound.
Red hot papa, it makes my love come down.

If you want me for your own,
Kiss me nice and leave me alone.
It makes my love come down, it makes my love come down.
Take me bye-bye, it makes my love come down.

When you take me for a ride,
When I'm close up by your side,
It makes my love come down, ridin' all around,
Easy ridin' makes my love come down.

Love in Vain

by Robert Johnson

Recorded by: Robert Johnson

When the train rolled up to the station, I looked her in the eye.(2X)
Well, I was lonesome, I felt so lonesome, and I could not help but cry.
All my love's in vain.

When the train, it left the station, with two lights on behind.(2X)
Well, the blue light was my blues, and the red light was my mind.
All my love's in vain.

Behind Closed Doors

Recorded by: Arthur Crudup

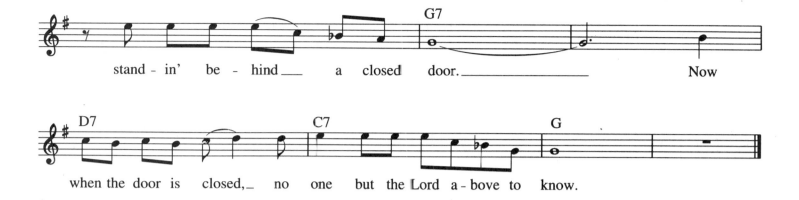

stand - in' be - hind ___ a closed door. _____ Now

when the door is closed,_ no one but the Lord a - bove to know.

When I first met you, baby, you was behind a closed door.(2X)
You know I was beggin' and beggin' you, make me a pallet on your floor.

Darling, you know I love you, I love you for myself.
Don't was you to fool around and find somebody else.
I don't want you, baby, standing behind a closed door.

Cry Your Blues Away

by Arthur 'Big Boy' Crudup

Recorded by: Arthur Crudup

Dar - ling, un - veil your face,___ go on and cry your blues_ a - way. ___

Dar - ling, un - veil your face,___ go on and cry your blues_ a - way. ___

___ You know I'm so glad_ trou - ble don't last_ al - ways.

Remember you told me I would never hear you say.(2X)
That is the reason, darling, why I can't say goodbye.

I'm gonna find someone to love me, someone I can call my own.(2X)
You know, I'm so tired of staying in this world alone.

Darling, you don't want me, you really treat me like a slave.(2X)
You know, some of these mornings I'll be dead and in my grave.

She Ain't Nothing but Trouble

by Arthur Big Boy Crudup

Recorded by: Arthur Crudup

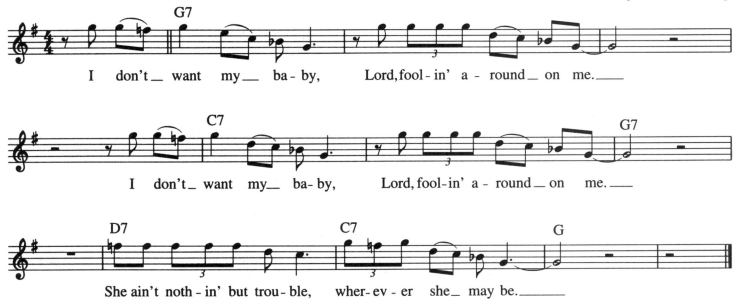

I don't__ want my__ ba- by, Lord, fool-in' a - round__ on me.__

I don't__ want my__ ba- by, Lord, fool-in' a - round__ on me.__

She ain't noth - in' but trou- ble, wher- ev- er she__ may be._____

Darlin', you ain't nothin in the world but trouble, I love you just the same.(2X)
I don't want my baby talkin' to another man.

Take me, darlin', hold me in your arms.
Love me, baby, love me all night long.
You ain't nothin' in the world but trouble, wherever she may be.

Now when the sun starts risin', Lord, I'm wringin' my hands and cryin'.(2X)
I love you, baby, I just can't get you off my mind.

If You Want Me to Love You

Recorded by: Tampa Red

You want me to love you, here's what you got to do.

You want me to love you,__ and make you__ love me too.

I got to have__ my lov- in'__ when my hab- its get __ old, __

Em or at nine in the eve-nin', love me **C7** all night **B7** long.___

Em You want me to love you,___ **C7** that's what you got___ **Em** to do.___

If you want me to love you, there's another thing you got to do.
If you want me to love you, and make you love me too.
If I wake up at night and I won't sleep, it's up to you to get me some of that Western beef.
If you want me to love you, that's what you got to do.

If you want me to love you, there's another thing you got to do.
If you want me to love you, and make you love me too.
You got to take all your money, throw it against the wall, you take what sticks and I'll take what falls.
If you want me to love you, that's the thing you got to do.

If you want me to love you, last thing you got to do.
If you want me to love you and make you love me too.
Take a butcher knife, cut off your head, send me a telegram that your body's dead.
If you want me to love you, that's what you got to do.

Someday

by Arthur Big Boy Crudup

Recorded by: Arthur Crudup

G7 Some-day, ba-by,___ some,___ some old lone-some day, Some-day,

C9 ba-by,___ some,___ some old lone-some **G** day,_____ **Am7** You

D7 know I won't be wor-ried **C9** and treat-ed this-a **G** way._____

When I go in my room, I fall down on my knees and pray.(2X)
That I have someone to love me, and I wish that you were there.

I have found somebody, some woman that really cares for me.(2X)
I mean I found a woman who wants to be my honey bee.

Dust My Broom
I Believe I'll

by Robert Johnson

Recorded by: Robert Johnson
Freddie King
Johnny Shines

I'm gon' get up in the morn-in',__ I be - lieve I'll dust __ my broom. __

I'm gon' get up in the morn- in',__ I be - lieve I'll dust my broom. _

__ Girl - friend, the black man you been lov - in', _____

girl - friend, can get my room. _____

I'm gon' write a letter, telephone every town I know.(2X)
If I can't find her in West Helena, she must be in East Monroe, I know.

I don't want no woman, wants every downtown man she meet.(2X)
She's a no good doney, they shouldn't 'low her on the street.

I believe, I believe I'll go back home.(2X)
You can mistreat me here, babe, but you can't when I go home.

And I'm gettin' up in the morning, I believe I'll dust my broom.(2X)
Girlfriend, the black man that you been lovin', girlfriend, can get my room.

I'm gon' call up Chiney, she is my good girl over there.(2X)
If I can't find her on Philippine's Island, she must be in Ethiopia somewhere.

Used by Permission of King of Spades Music

When You Got a Good Friend

by Robert Johnson

Recorded by: Robert Johnson

When you got a good __ friend, __ that will stay right by your side. _

__ When you got __ a good friend, __

Used by Permission of King of Spades Music

that will stay right your side. _____ Give her

all of your spare_ time, love and treat her right. _

I mistreat my baby, and I can't see no reason why.(2X)
Every time I think about it, I just wring my hands and cry.

Wonder, could I bear apologize, or would she sympathize with me.
Mmm, would she sympathize with me.
She's a brownskin woman, just as sweet as a girlfriend can be.

Mmm, babe, I may be right or wrong.
Baby, it your opinion, I may be right or wrong.
Watch your close friend, baby, you enemies can't do you no harm.

When you got a good friend that will stay right by your side.(2X)
Give her all of your spare time, love and treat her right.

Dark and Dreary

by Joe Josea and Elmore James

Recorded by: Elmore James

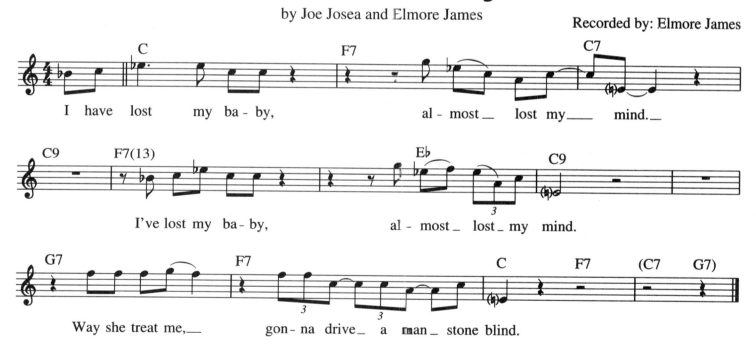

I have lost my ba - by, al - most _ lost my ___ mind. _

I've lost my ba - by, al - most _ lost _ my mind.

Way she treat me, _ gon - na drive _ a man _ stone blind.

Well, the road seemed dark and dreary, while I traveled down that way.(2X)
Well, my baby left me, she just come back home today.

Oh, I love my baby, tell the world I do.(2X)
Well, I need a little lovin', darlin', gonna make my dream come true.

Oh, I love you darlin', like a schoolboy loves his pie.(2X)
Now ain't that the way to treat me, darlin', my hurt's so long that I will die.

Run and Tell Your Daddy

Recorded by: Charlie Jordan

They say ev' - ry-thing I tell you, you run and tell your dad- dy, Lord. _

Ev'- thing I tell you, run tell your dad- dy, Lord. _ They say ev' -

'ry thing I tell you, you run and tell you dad dy, Lord. _

I ain't gonna tell you nothin' else, cause run and tell your daddy, Lord.(3X)

Everything I give you, you give it to your daddy, Lord.(3X).

Dog jumped a rabbit, run him for a solid mile.(2X)
Well, he said he couldn't catch it, so he tried just like a natural child.

Sister was a cheetah, your daddy was a great big bear.(2X)
Well, rope around my neck, lead me anywhere.

Gambler's Blues

by Hopkins and Lewis

Recorded by: Lightning Hopkins

You know I once __ was a gam - bler, __ I bet and lost my

mon- ey soon. Yes, I once was a gam- bler, boy, but I

lost my mon- ey soon. __ Yes. I lost __ all my mon - ey some oth- er,

some oth- er gam - bler can have my room. __

You know I lost all my money in her no good gambling game.(2X)
I was on my bad luck, kept gambling just the same.

Man, when you lose that old no good money, sit around with your head hung down.(2X)
Yeah, wake up the next morning, I'm the best gambler in this town.

Natural Ball

by Aaron T. Bone Walker

Recorded by : T. Bone Walker

Let your hair down, ba-by, let's have a nat-ur-al ball.

Let your hair down, ba-by,

let's have a nat-'ral ball. 'Cause when you

aint hap-py, ba-by, ain't no fun at all.

Well, you can't take it with you, that's one thing for sure.(2X)
Well, you know I love you, baby, but I can't use you no more.

Come on home, pretty baby, spend my love with you.(2X)
Well, you mess with me, pretty mama, don't like the way you do.

Little Queen of Spades

by Robert Johnson

Recorded by: Robert Johnson

Now she is a lit-tle queen of spades,

and the men will not let her be.

Hoo, she's the lit-tle queen of spades,

and the men will not ____ let her be. ____

Ev'- ry time she makes_ a spread,_ hoo, fair

brown, cold chills just run all o - ver me.____

I'm gon' get me a gamblin' woman, if it's the last thing that I do.(2X)
Well, a man don't need a woman, hoo fair brown, that he got to give all his money to.

Everybody say she got a mojo, now she's been using that stuff.(2X)
But she got a way of trimmin' down, hoo fair brown, and I mean it's most too tough.

Now, little girl, since I am the king, baby, and you is a queen.(2X)
Let us put our head together, hoo fair brown, then we make our money green.

Can't Stop Lovin'

by Elmore James

Recorded by: Elmore James

I can't stop lov- in', _____ my ba- by to - night._

I can't stop lov- in', _____ my ba- by to - night. _

No mat-ter what I do, she won't treat me right._

I loved my baby, this mornin' soon.(2X)
I didn't come back home till this afternoon.

When I leave my baby, she's all alone.(2X)
I can't have no lovin', cause my baby's gone.

Oh, baby, come and walk with me.(2X)
I'll make you happy, baby, as any girl can be.

Oh, baby, come all alone.(2X)
I hope someday, baby, you will come back home.

32-20 Blues

by Robert Johnson

Recorded by: Robert Johnson
Skip James
Willie Kelly

I sent ___ for my ba - by, and she don't come. I sent ___

___ for my ba - by, man, and she don't come. All the doc-

tors in Hot Springs sure ___ can't help ___ her none. ___

And if she gets unruly, thinks she don't want do.(2X)
Take my 32-20, and cut her half in two.

She got a thirty-eight special, but I believe it's most too light.(2X)
I got a 32-20, got to make the camps alright.

If I send for my baby, man, and she don't come.(2X)
All the doctors in Hot Springs sure can't help her none.

I'm gonna shoot my pistol, gonna shoot my Gatlin' gun.(2X)
You made me love you, now your man done come.

Ah baby, where you stay last night?(2X)
You got your hair all tangles, and you ain't talkin' right.

Got a thirty-eight special, boys, it do very well.

I Wonder Why

by B.B. King and Joe Josea

Recorded by: Freddie King

I won - der why ___ my ba - by won't treat me right. ___

I won - der why ___ my ba - by won't

treat me right. __   She's a   mean, __   mean wom - an,

and she don't come home _ last night. __

She's a gamblin' woman, she chases me in between.(2X)
Yes, she's a mean, mean woman, the meanest woman I ever seen.

I'll be home late last Friday, that's what you said.(2X)
Yes, the way my baby treats me, sometimes I wish I was dead.

I get in my bed, I lie awake in broad daylight.(2X)
Yes, I'll be laying one moment, will my baby be home tonight.

Why Won't My Baby Treat Me Right

by Aaron 'T. Bone' Walker

Recorded by: T. Bone Walker

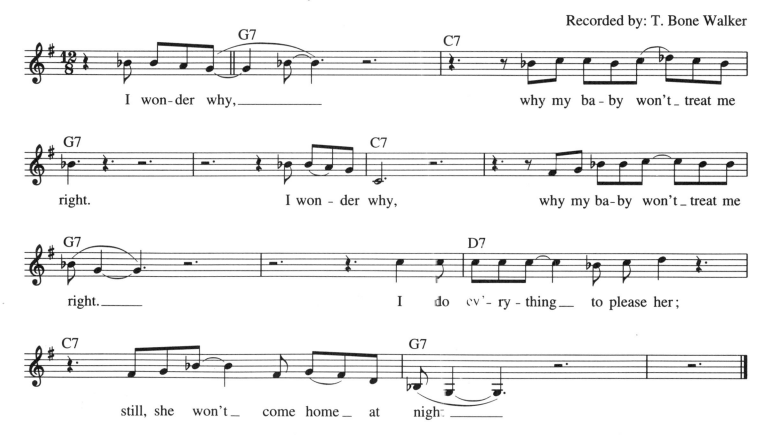

I won-der why, _____   why my ba - by won't _ treat me

right.   I won - der why,   why my ba - by won't _ treat me

right. _____   I   do ev'- ry - thing __ to please her;

still, she won't _ come home _ at   night _____

"I'll be home," way last week, that's what she said.(2X)
She don't care if I don't eat, and she don't know how to rest me in bed.

Gamblin' woman, and she spends in between.(2X)
She's a dirty mistreater, meanest girl I ever seen.

Walking Blues

by Robert Johnson

Recorded by: Robert Johnson

I woke up this morn-in', _____ feel-in' round for my shoes.

Know by that __ I got these old walk-in' blues, well. Woke this mor-nin' __

feel 'round for my shoes. __ But you know __

__ by that, __ I got these __ old walk-in' blues.

Well, leave this mornin' if I have to, ride the blinds.
I feel mistreated, and I don't mind dyin'.
Leave this morning, if I have to ride the blind.
Babe, I been mistreated, and I don't mind dyin'.

Well, some people tell me that the worried blues ain't bad.
Worst old feelin' I most ever had.
People tell me that these old worried blues ain't bad.
It's the worst old feelin', I most ever had.

She got a elgin movement from her head down to her toes.
Break in on a dollar most anywhere she goes.
Ooh, to her head down to her toes.
Lord, she break in on a dollar, most anywhere she goes.

That's Why I'm Lonesome

by Arthur Big Boy Crudup

Recorded by: Arthur Crudup

Half-time feel

Well, I've got no one to love me, guess I'm all a - lone,

That's why I'm wor-ried, dar-ling, and I'm all a - lone. You know I'm

wor - ried,_____ yes, I'm lone - some._____ You know I'm lone - some

ba - by,_____ in this world for you._____

Sometimes I'm on the wonder, wonder to myself.
You know I love you, baby, and you love somebody else.
But I am wondering, yes, I'm wondering.
You know I'm wondering, baby, in this world for you.

I ain't got nobody, I'm here all alone.
The one I love, she really don't stay at home.
That's why I'm lonesome, yes, I'm lonesome.
You know I'm lonesome, baby, in this world for you.

Sporting Life Blues

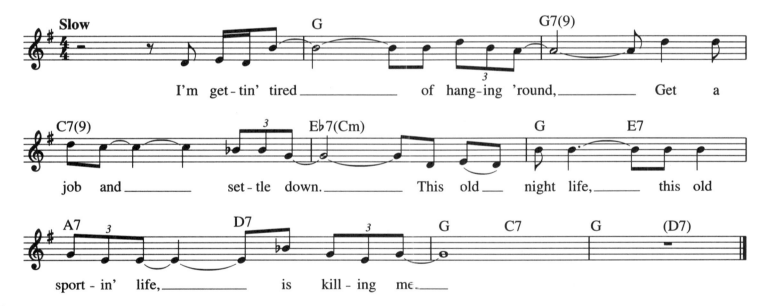

I'm get - tin' tired_____ of hang - ing 'round,_____ Get a

job and_____ set - tle down._____ This old__ night life,_____ this old

sport - in' life,_____ is kill - ing me.____

I got a letter from my home,
Most of my friends are dead and gone.
This old night life, this old sportin' life,
Is killing me.

There ain't but one thing that I've done wrong,
Lived this sportin' life too long.
This old night life, this old sportin' life,
Is killing me.

I've been a liar, and a cheater too,
Spent all of my money and my booze on you.
This old night life, this old sportin' life,
Is killing me.

I'm getting tired of running around,
I think I'll marry and settle down.
This old night life, this old sportin' life,
Is killing me.

Bad Breaks

Recorded by: B.B. King

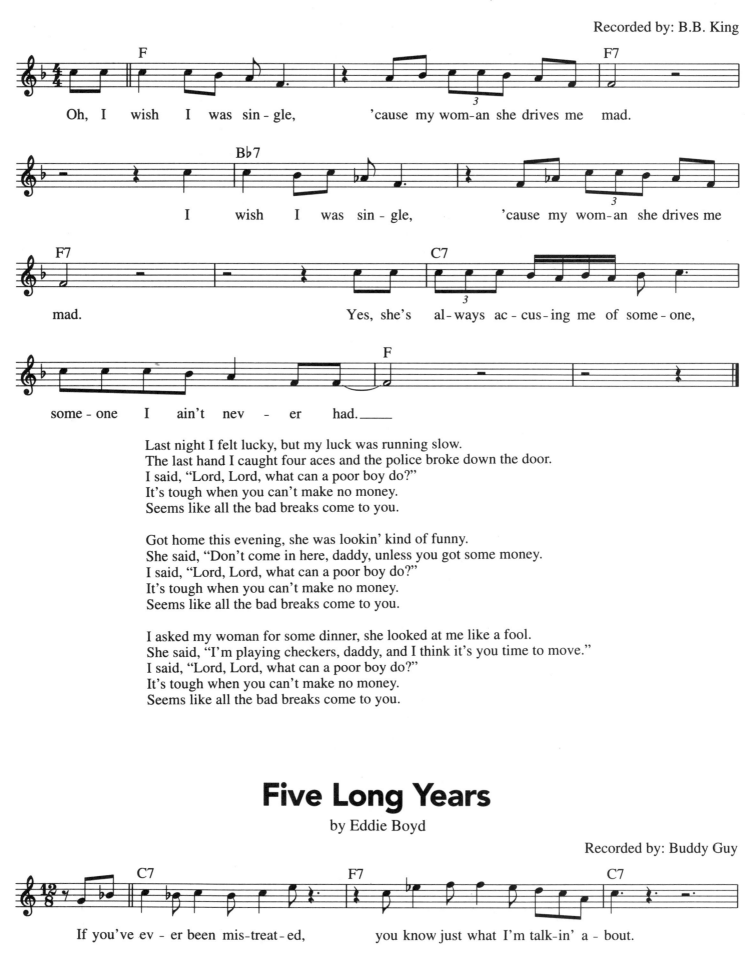

Oh, I wish I was sin - gle, 'cause my wom-an she drives me mad.

I wish I was sin - gle, 'cause my wom-an she drives me

mad. Yes, she's al - ways ac - cus-ing me of some - one,

some - one I ain't nev - er had.____

Last night I felt lucky, but my luck was running slow.
The last hand I caught four aces and the police broke down the door.
I said, "Lord, Lord, what can a poor boy do?"
It's tough when you can't make no money.
Seems like all the bad breaks come to you.

Got home this evening, she was lookin' kind of funny.
She said, "Don't come in here, daddy, unless you got some money.
I said, "Lord, Lord, what can a poor boy do?"
It's tough when you can't make no money.
Seems like all the bad breaks come to you.

I asked my woman for some dinner, she looked at me like a fool.
She said, "I'm playing checkers, daddy, and I think it's you time to move."
I said, "Lord, Lord, what can a poor boy do?"
It's tough when you can't make no money.
Seems like all the bad breaks come to you.

Five Long Years

by Eddie Boyd

Recorded by: Buddy Guy

If you've ev - er been mis-treat-ed, you know just what I'm talk-in' a - bout.

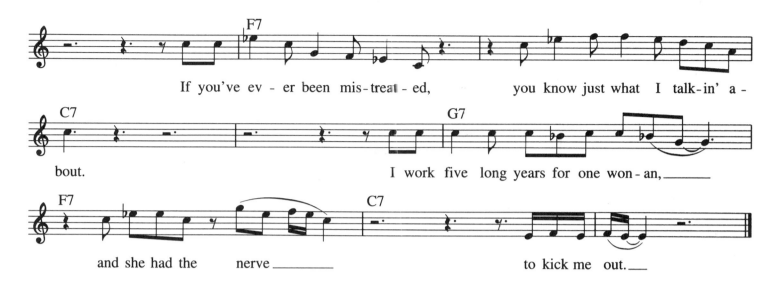

If you've ev-er been mis-treat-ed, you know just what I talk-in' a-bout. I work five long years for one wom-an,_____ and she had the nerve_____ to kick me out.__

I got a job at a steel mill, truckin' steel just like a slave.
Five long years of fright I'm runnin', straight home with all of my pay.
Mistreated, you know what I'm talkin' about?
I work five long years for one woman, and she had the nerve to throw me out.

Shake That Thing

Recorded by: Papa Charlie Jackson

Now, the old folks like it, and the young folks too.__ The old folks tell the young_ folks how to do.__ You gon-na shake that thing, aw, shake that thing.__ I'm get-tin' sick and tired_ of tell-in' you to shake __ that thing.__

Now, it ain't no Johnson, ain't no chicken wings.
All you got to do is to shake that thing.
Why don't you shake that thing, shake that thing.
I'm getting sick and tired of telling you to shake that thing.

I was walking downtown and stumbled and fell.
My mouth jumped open like a front wheel well.
Why don't you shake that thing, shake that thing.
I'm getting sick and tired of telling you to shake that thing.

Sweet Home Chicago

by Robert Johnson

Recorded by: Robert Johnson

Now, one and one is two, two and two is four.
I'm heavy loaded, baby, I'm booked, I gotta go.
Cryin' baby, honey, don't you want to go,
Back to the land of California, to my sweet home Chicago.

Now two and two is four, four and two is six.
You gon' keep on monkeyin' 'round here, friend-boy, you gon' get your business all in a trick.
I'm cryin' baby, honey, don't you want to go,
Back to the land of California, to my sweet home Chicago.

Now six and two is eight, eight and two is ten.
Friend-boy, she trick you one time, sure she gon' do it again.
I'm cryin' hey, hey, baby, don't you want to go,
To the land of California, to my sweet home Chicago.

I'm goin' to California, from there to Des Moines, Iowa.
Somebody will tell me that you need my help someday.
Cryin' hey, hey, baby, don't you want to go,
Back to the land of California, to my sweet home Chicago.

Used by Permission of King of Spades Music

Memphis Slim

You'll Like My Loving

Recorded by: Otis Harris

I know you like __ my __ lov - in', I can tell __
__ from the way you whine. __ I know you like __ my
lov - in', I can tell __ from the way you whine. __
Let you taste my jel - ly, you just wor-ries me all the __ time. __

I told you, pretty mama, I had the best jelly in town.(2X)
Since you got a little taste, you just keep on hanging around.

I swim deep, pretty mama, just like a catfish loaded down.(2X)
And every time you see me, you wants to fall down on the ground.

When me and my baby starts to lovin', we wants to fight like cats and dogs.(2X)
But before it's over with, we hollerin', "Lord, oh, Lordy Lord."

As Long as I Have You

by Willie Dixon

Recorded by: Willie Dixon

Long as I have you, __ long as I have you, __
noth-ing I would-n't do, ba - by, long as I have you. __

Well, I don't mind work-ing, I'll be your slave, _ just call me, ba- by, and I'll rise from my grave._ Long as I have you. long as I have you, _ noth- ing I would - n't do, ba- by, long as I have you. _

I'll do like a lizard,
I'll drag in the sand,
Just call me sweet names,
And I'll be your man.
Long as I have you,
Long as I have you,
Nothing I wouldn't do, baby,
Long as I have you.

Mean and Evil

Recorded by: Elmore James

My ba- by's so mean. and e- vil,_ I don't know what to do. _

My ba- by's so mean_ and e- vil,_ I don't_ know what to do.

Treat me low down and dirt - y, well, I can't _ get a - long with you.

When we lived in a small town, you was nice and neat.(2X)
I brought you to Chicago, you do nothin' but walk the street.

Well, she used to cook my breakfast and bring it to my bed.
She used to wash my face and even comb my hair.
She's so evil I don't know what to do.
You treat me so low down and dirty,
And I can't get along with you.

No Matter How She Done it

Recorded by: Tampa Red

I know a gal___ by the name of Mae - Lou.___ She

shook it so much_ she had the Ger-man flu.___ No mat-ter how she done it,

No mat-ter how she done it, No

mat-ter how she done it, She done it just the same.

The women don't like her, they call her Ida Mae,
But the way the men love her is a cryin' shame.

chorus

I tell you people what she done,
She made a hit with Jack the Ripper, and the only one.

chorus

You women don't have to worry 'bout your life,
She made Jack the Ripper throw away his knife.

chorus

She shakes all over when she walks.
She made a blind man see, and a dumb man talk.

chorus

The copper brought her in, she didn't need no bail.
She shook it for the judge, and put the cop in jail.

chorus

Farewell to You Baby

Recorded by: Carl Martin

I'm leav- in' you ba - by, __ it's be- cause you won't be true. __

I'm leav- in' you ba - by, it's be - cause __ you won't be

true. Lord, __ you don't love me, ___

af - ter all ___ I done __ for you

You know, I worked hard all winter when the snow was on the ground.(2X)
You mistreated me then, baby, still I wouldn't throw you down

You made mistakes, baby, after you made your vow.(2X)
But your mischief making is all over now.

You goin' to miss your daddy some old lonesome day, and you goin' to be sorry you did me this way.
You gonna miss me, some old lonesome day,
And you goin' to be sorry you did me this a way.

Now I'm leavin' you baby, with my clothes in my hand, might well do you, baby, get yourself a monkey man.
I'm leavin', with my clothes in my hand.
Farewell to you, get yourself a monkey man.

Trouble No More

Written by Muddy Waters

Recorded by: Muddy Waters

I don't care _ how long you're gone, I don't care _ how long you stay, but good time treat-ment _ gon' bring you home _ some day. _ But some day, ba - by, ain't gon' trou - ble _ poor _ me an - y more.

You just keep on setting that the dice don't pass,
Well, you know, darling, you are living too fast.

I'm gonna tell everybody in your neighborhood,
That you the sweet little girl, but you don't mean me no good.

Well, I know you're leaving, you call that gone,
Well, without love, you can't stay long.

Well, goodbye, baby, yeah, shake my hand,
I don't want no woman, you can have a man.

Candy Man Blues

Recorded by: Mississippi John Hurt

All _ you lad - ies gath - er _ 'round, the good sweet _ can - dy man's in town. _ Can - dy man, _ Can - dy man. _

Hey, Pretty Mama

by Willie Dixon

2. Now tell me, baby, if your love is true,
Time past so fast when I'm loving you
Now tell me, baby, if I love you too strong,
When I get in the mood, I can roll all night long.

Traveling Riverside Blues

by Robert Johnson

Recorded by: Robert Johnson

If your man ___ gets per - son - al, want to have your fun. ___

If your man ___ gets per - son - al, ___

want to have your fun. ___ Just come on

back to Friar's ___ Point, ma - ma, and bar - rel - house all night long. ___

I got women in Vicksburg, clean on into Tennessee.(2X)
But my Friar's Point rider, now, hops all over me.

I ain't gon' to state no color, but her front teeth crowned with gold.(2X)
She got a mortgage on my body, now, and a lien on my soul.

Lord, I'm goin' to Rosedale, gon' take my rider by my side.(2X)
We can still barrelhouse, baby, 'cause it's on the river side.

Now you can squeeze my lemon till the juice run down my...
(*Spoken:* Till the juice run down my leg, baby, you know what I'm talkin' 'bout.)
You can squeeze my lemon till the juice run down my leg.
But I'm goin' back to Friar's Point, if I be rockin' to my head.

Matchbox Blues

Recorded by: Blind Lemon Jefferson

I'm sit - tin' here ___ won - d'ring, ___ will a match-box hold ___ my clothes. ___

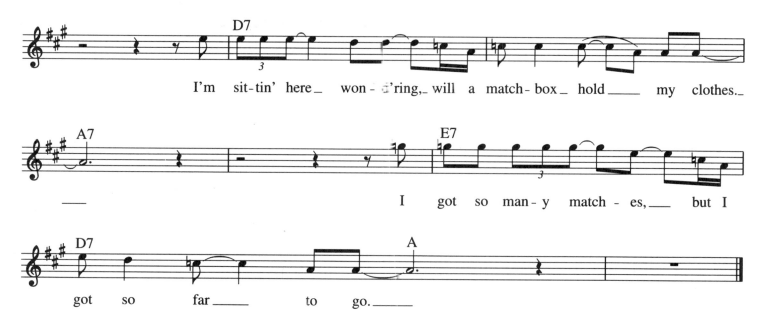

I'm sit-tin' here __ won-d'ring, __ will a match-box __ hold __ my clothes. __

__ I got so man-y match-es, __ but I

got so far __ to go. __

Walk Right In

( ) = alternate chord changes

Recorded by: Gus Cannon

Walk right in, __ sit right down, __ and ba-by, let your mind roll

on. __ Hey, walk right in, __ stay a-while, __ but

dad-dy you __ been stayin' too long. __ Now, ev'-ry bod-y's talk-in' 'bout a

new way of walk-in'. do you want to lose your mind? __ Hey,

walk right in, __ sit right down, __ dad-dy let your mind roll on.

Walking My Troubles Away

Recorded by: Blind Boy Fuller

Pa - per boy __ hol- lerin', "Ex - tra, have you read the news?"

Shot the brown I love, I got them walk - ing blues. I keep on

walk - ing, _____ trying to walk _ my trou - bles a - way. _

I'm _ so glad, _____ trou - ble don't last al - ways. _

You used to be my sweet hip, you soured on me.
We won't be together like we used to be.
I keep on walking, trying to walk my trouble away.
I'm so glad, trouble don't last always.

I got the bad luck blues, my bad luck time done come.
They said bad luck follow everybody, seem like I'm the only one.
I keep on walking, trying to walk my trouble away.
I'm so glad, trouble don't last always.

I Asked for Water

by Chester Burnett

Recorded by: Howlin' Wolf

Oh, _____ asked her for wa - ter, _____

Oh, _____ she brought me gas - o - line. ___

Oh, ___ asked her for wa - ter, ___

Oh _____ she brought me gas - o - line. _____

Just the ter - ri - bl'st wom - an _____

that I ev - er seen. __

Tom Rushen Blues

Recorded by: Charlie Patton

Laid down last night,___ hop-in' I would___ have my peace, eee._____ I laid down last night,___ hop-in' I would have my peace, ___ eee._____ But when I woke up, Tom Rush-en was __ shak-in' me. ___

When you get in trouble, it's no use to screamin' and cryin'.(2X)
Tom Rushen will take you back to the prison house flyin'.

It were late one night, Halloway was gone to bed.(2X)
Mister Day brought whiskey taken from under Halloway's head.

An' it's boozey booze, now, Lord, to cure these blues.(2X)
But each day seems like years in the jailhouse where there is no boo'.

I got up this mornin', Tom Day was standin' around.(2X)
If he lose his office now, he's runnin' from town to town.

Let me tell you folksies just how he treated me.(2X)
Aw, he caught me yellin', I was drunk as I could be.

Wild About You Baby

by Elmore James

Recorded by: Elmore James

Well, I'm wild a-bout you, ba - by,___ and you just won't treat me

right.

Yes, I'm wild a-bout you, ba - by,___

and you just won't treat me right.___

You leave home ear - ly in the morn - ing,

and stays out all___ day long.___

Devil Got My Woman

by Nehemiah 'Skip' James

Recorded by: Skip James

minor tonality throughout

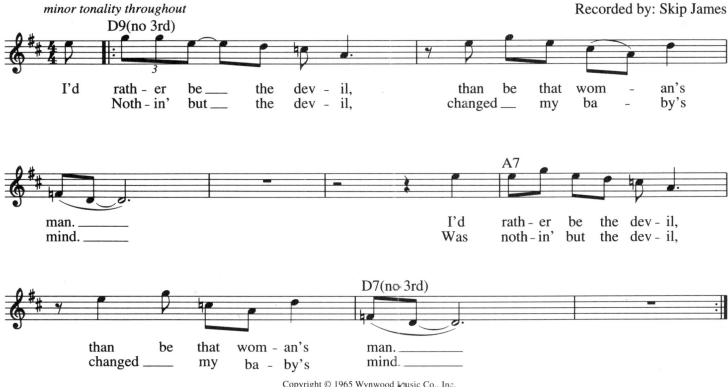

I'd rath - er be___ the dev - il, than be that wom - an's
Noth - in' but___ the dev - il, changed___ my ba - by's

man._____ I'd rath - er be the dev - il,
mind._____ Was noth - in' but the dev - il,

than be that wom - an's man._____
changed___ my ba - by's mind._____

Good Liquor Gonna Carry Me Down

Recorded by: Big Bill Broonzy

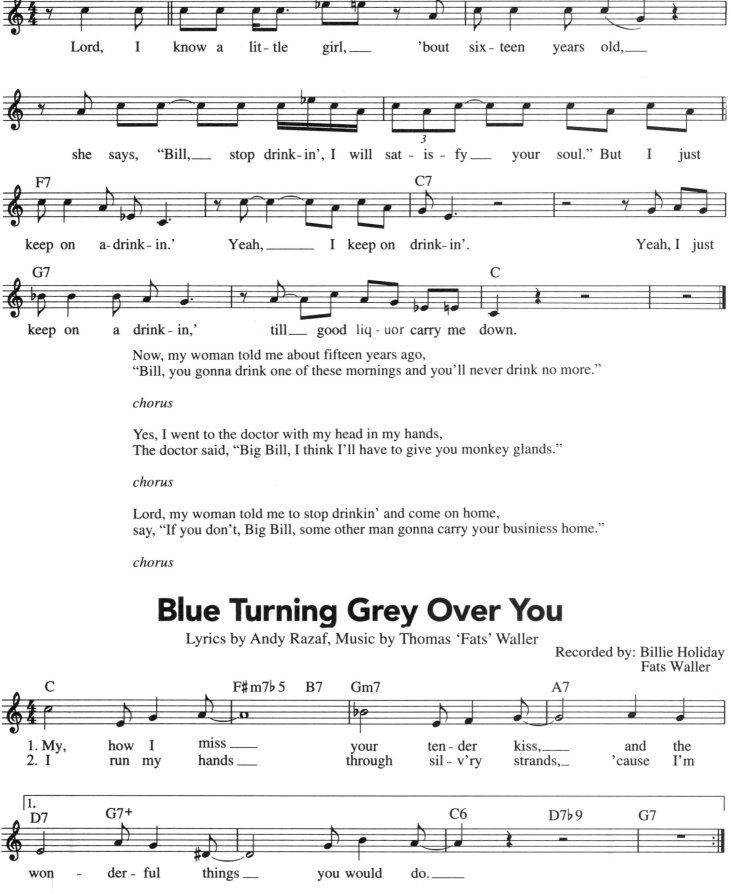

Now, my woman told me about fifteen years ago,
"Bill, you gonna drink one of these mornings and you'll never drink no more."

chorus

Yes, I went to the doctor with my head in my hands,
The doctor said, "Big Bill, I think I'll have to give you monkey glands."

chorus

Lord, my woman told me to stop drinkin' and come on home,
say, "If you don't, Big Bill, some other man gonna carry your businiess home."

chorus

Blue Turning Grey Over You

Lyrics by Andy Razaf, Music by Thomas 'Fats' Waller

Recorded by: Billie Holiday
Fats Waller

|2.
D7   **G7+**   **C6**   **F**   **G7**

blue turn - ing grey___ o - ver you.___

C7   **F**   **Dm7**   **C**   **C7**

You used to be___ so good to me,___

F   **Am7**   **D7**   **G**   **D9**

that's when I was___ a nov - el - ty. Now you have

C   **F#m7♭5 B7**   **Gm7**   **A7**

new thrills in view,___ found some - one new,___ left me

D9   **G7+**   **C**   **(D7**   **G7**   **G7+)**

blue turn - ing grey___ o - ver you.___

One Dime Blues

Recorded by: Blind Lemon Jefferson

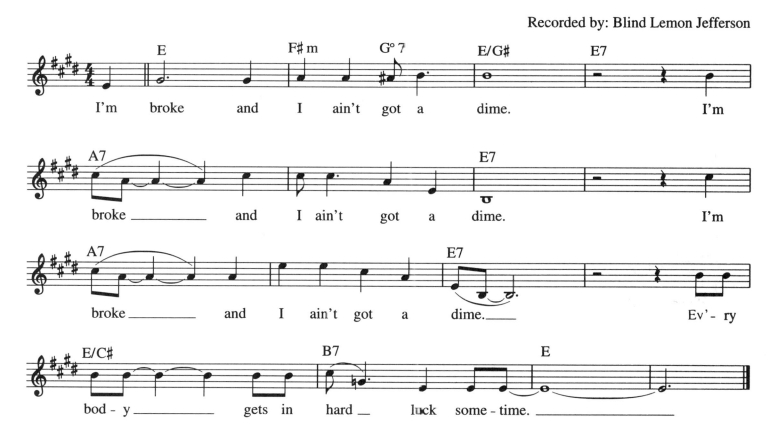

E   **F#m**   **G°7**   **E/G#**   **E7**

I'm broke and I ain't got a dime. I'm

A7   **E7**

broke _____ and I ain't got a dime. I'm

A7   **E7**

broke _____ and I ain't got a dime.___ Ev' - ry

E/C#   **B7**   **E**

bod - y _____ gets in hard _ luck some - time. _____

Please Warm My Wiener

Recorded by: Bo Carter

I got some-thin' to tell you, ba- by, don't get mad this time, If you want my wie-ner you gim-me, he's all up in __ my mind. Ba-by, please warm my wien - er, ba - by please warm my wien - er. Won't you just warm my wien - er, 'cause he real - ly don't feel right cold.

Now listen here, sweet baby, I ain't no lyin' man,
If you warm my wiener one time you'll want to warm him again.
Baby, please warm my wiener, oh, warm my wiener.
Won't you just warm my wiener, 'cause he really don't feel right cold.

Says some say to take hot water, baby can't you see,
But your heat, baby, is plenty warm enough for me.
Baby, please warm my wiener, please warm my wiener.
Won't you just warm my wiener, 'cause he really don't feel right cold.

Now listen here, sweet baby, you know that time is growing old,
I don't want you to warm half of my wiener, I want you to warm him all.
Baby, please warm my wiener, baby please warm my wiener.
Won't you warm my wiener, 'cause he really don't feel right cold.

Bring it With You When You Come

Recorded by: Gus Cannon

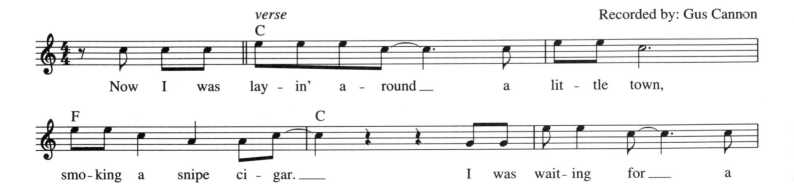

Now I was lay - in' a - round __ a lit - tle town, smo-king a snipe ci - gar. __ I was wait-ing for __ a

D7 G7
hand - out, just to catch an emp - ty car. Just as the
C C7 F
freight train came roll - ing by, my wait was all in vain.
C F C
Back off, back off, you dir - ty bum, and
D7 G7 C
catch the next freight train. Now, if you
chorus
C F C
wan - na be a lit - tle girl of mine, bring it with you when you come.
D7
Played a - round the lit - tle town, your head chock full of rum.
G7 C C/B♭
I can't send you down - town for too lit - tle sap, now,
F/A Fm/A♭ C
she's sit - ting on an - oth - er man's lap. Now, you want to be a
F D7 G7 C
girl of mine, bring it with you when you come.

Michigan Water Blues

Recorded by: Jelly Roll Morton

Mich-i-gan ___ wa - ter tastes like sher - ry

wine, I mean sher - ry wine. ___ Oh, the Mis - sis - sip - pi wa - ter.

tastes like tur - pen - tine. ___ Mich-i-gan wa - ter

tastes like sher - ry wine. ___

Believe to my soul that girl's got a black cat bone, yes, a black cat bone.
She'll go away but she'll surely come back home.
Michigan water tastes like sherry wine.

She looks like frog, hops like a kangaroo.
If you ain't got no hopper, she'll be your hopper too.
Michigan water tastes like sherry wine.
Michigan water tastes like sherry wine.

Gal in Alabama, one in Spain,
Another in Mississippi, I'm scared to call her name.
Michigan water tastes like sherry wine.
Michigan water tastes like sherry wine.

Basin Street Blues

by Spencer Williams

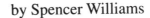

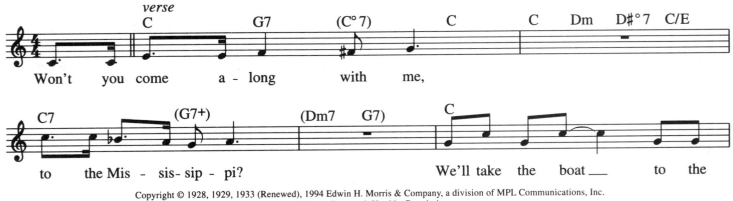

Won't you come a - long with me,

to the Mis - sis - sip - pi? We'll take the boat ___ to the

165

How Do You Want it Done

Recorded by: Big Bill Broonzy

Double time feel

Why don't you tell me, lov-in' ma-ma, how you want _____ you roll-in'___ done?

Why don't you tell me, lov-in' ma-ma, how you want ____ you roll-in'_ done?

Lord, I give you sat-is-fac-tion, now, if _____ it's all night _ long.

Lord, I got up this morning just about the break of day.(2X)
Lord, I'm thinkin' 'bout my baby, Lord, the one that went away.

I got me a little brownskin, just as sweet as she can be.(2X)
Lord, she low and she is squatty, but she's alright with me.

Now you can put me in the alley, my gal's name is Sally,
You wake me up in the mornin', mama, I still got that old habit.
Why don't you tell me, how you want it done.
Now, I give you satisfaction, now if it's all night long.

Lord, some of these old mornings, mama, Lord, it won't be long.(2X)
Lord, I know you gonna call me, mama, Lord, and I'll be there.

Memphis Blues

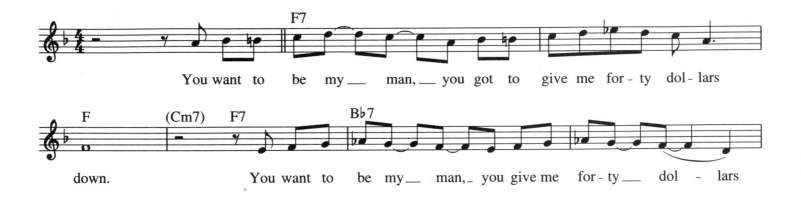

You want to be my __ man, __ you got to give me for-ty dol-lars down.

You want to be my__ man,_ you give me for-ty __ dol-lars

down.   If you won't be my___ man,___ your

ba - by's gon - na shake this   tow—.   Mis - ter

Crump don't   'low___   no eas - y rid   - ers here.

Crump don't   'low___   no eas - y rid   - ers here.

We don't _ care _ what Mis - ter Crump don't 'low.___ We gon - na bar-rel-house

an - y   how.___ Mis - ter Crump don't 'low___ no eas - y rid - ers

here.   I'm go- in'   down the riv - er, go-in' down to the riv - er, gonna
                         Mis - sis - sip-pi Riv-er, Mis-sis-sip-pi,_____

take   my rock - in'   chair.____   Goin' down the   riv - er,_____
So   deep and   wide____   Mis - 'sip - pi   riv - er,_____

gon - na take my rock- in'   chair. __   Blues o - ver-take me
riv - er so___ deep and   wide. __   Man, I_____ love,___

gon - na rock a - way from   here. ___   Oh, the
he is on the oth - er   side. ___   ___

Pickpocket Blues

by Bessie Smith

Recorded by: Bessie Smith

Where Can My Baby Be

by Elmore James

Recorded by: Elmore James

Stealing

Recorded by: Memphis Jug Band

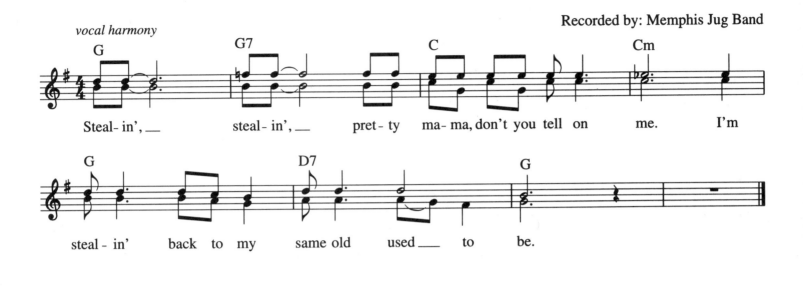

Steal-in', __ steal-in', __ pret-ty ma-ma, don't you tell on me. I'm

steal-in' back to my same old used __ to be.

Baby Doll

by Bessie Smith

Recorded by: Bessie Smith

Hon-ey, there's a fun-ny feel-ing 'round my heart, and it's

bound to drive your ma-ma wild. It must be some-thing they

call the Cu-ban doll, __ it weren't your ma-ma's an-gel child. I

went to see the doc-tor the oth-er day, he said I's well as well could

be: But I said, "Doc-tor, you don't know __

B. B. King

Shoe Shine Boy

Recorded by: Lester Young

When the Lights Go Out

Written by Willie Dixon

Recorded by: Jimmy Witherspoon

The Woman I Love

by B.B. King and Joe Josea

Recorded by: B.B. King

Weary Blues

Recorded by: Bessie Smith

Louis Collins

Recorded by: Mississippi John Hurt

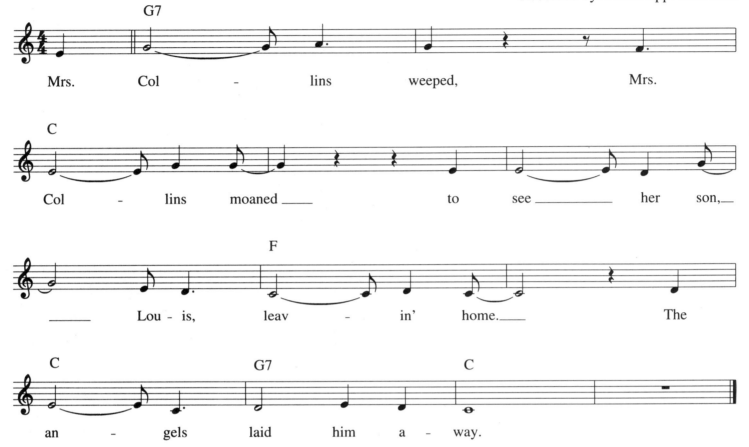

Mrs. Col - lins weeped, Mrs.
Col - lins moaned ___ to see ___ her son, ___
___ Lou - is, leav - in' home. ___ The
an - gels laid him a - way.

The angels laid him away,
They laid him six feet under the clay.
The angels laid him away.
Oh, Bob shot once and Louis shot two,

Shot poor Collins, shot him through and through.
The angels laid him away.
Oh, kind friends, oh, ain't it hard?
To see poor Louis in a new graveyard.

The angels laid him away.
Oh, when they heard that Louis was dead,
The angels laid him away.
All the people they dressed in red.

Johnny Winter, James Cotton, and Muddy Waters

Darlin' You Know I Love You

Recorded by: B.B. King

Now, dar - lin'_____ you know I love you _____ and love you _____ by my - self, But you've gone and left me for some - bod - y else. I think of you ev' - ry morn-in',_____ and dream of you ev' - ry night, And I would love to be with you al - ways. _____ When night _____ be - gins to fall, I

181

My Creole Belle

Recorded by: Mississippi John Hurt

My Creole belle, I love her well,
I love her more, anyone can tell.
My Creole belle, I love her well,
My darlin' baby, my Creole belle.

When the stars are shining, I'll call her mine,
My darlin' baby, my Creole belle.
My Creole belle, I love her well,
My darlin' baby, my Creole belle.

Time to Say Goodbye

Recorded by: B.B. King

There was a time _____ when I loved

you, _____ That was a time, babe, _____ you made me

blue. There's a time _____ ev' - ry - thing must end,

so now it's time to say we're through. _____

Remember the time, the time you made me cry,
But now, baby, you break my heart.
They say there's a time for everything, baby,
So now it's time we must part.

Remember the time, baby, you made me cry,
And the time, baby, when you broke my heart.
But there's a time for everything, baby,
So now it's time we must part.

They say that time brings about change,
And I know, baby, I know it is no lie,
There's times I got to forget you, baby,
So it's time to say goodbye

Richlands Woman Blues

Recorded by: Mississippi John Hurt

Come along young man, everything settin' right.
My husbands goin' away till next Saturday night.
Hurry down, sweet daddy, some blowin' your horn,
If you come too late, sweet mama will be gone.

Now I'm raring to go got red shoes on my feet.
My mind is sittin' right for a Tin Lizzie seat.
Hurry down, sweet daddy, come blowin' your horn,
If you come too late, sweet mama will be gone.

The red rooster said, "Cockle-doodle-do-do."
The Richlands' woman said, "Any dude will do."
Hurry down, sweet daddy, come blowin' your horn,
If you come too late, sweet mama will be gone.

With rosy red garters, pink hose on my feet,
Turkey red bloomer, with a rumble seat.
Hurry down, sweet daddy, come blowin' your horn,
If you come too late, sweet mama will be gone.

Every Sunday mornin', church people watch me go,
My wings sprouted out and the preacher told me so.
Hurry down, sweet daddy, come blowin' your horn,
If you come too late, sweet mama will be gone.

Dress skirt cut high, then they cut low,
Don't think I'm a sport, keep on watchin' me go.
Hurry down, sweet daddy, come blowin' your horn,
If you come too late, sweet mama will be gone.

Shake Yours

Recorded by: B.B. King

G7

Hel - lo, ba - by, I'm so glad to be back.__

C7

Got news for you, ba - by, that's a nat-'ral fact.__

G   D7   C7

Since I am back let's get in - to our act.__

G   G7

I love you, ba - by, more than words can say..

C7

You know I've missed you while I was a - way.

G   D7   C7

Now, come back, ba - by, __ now it's time to

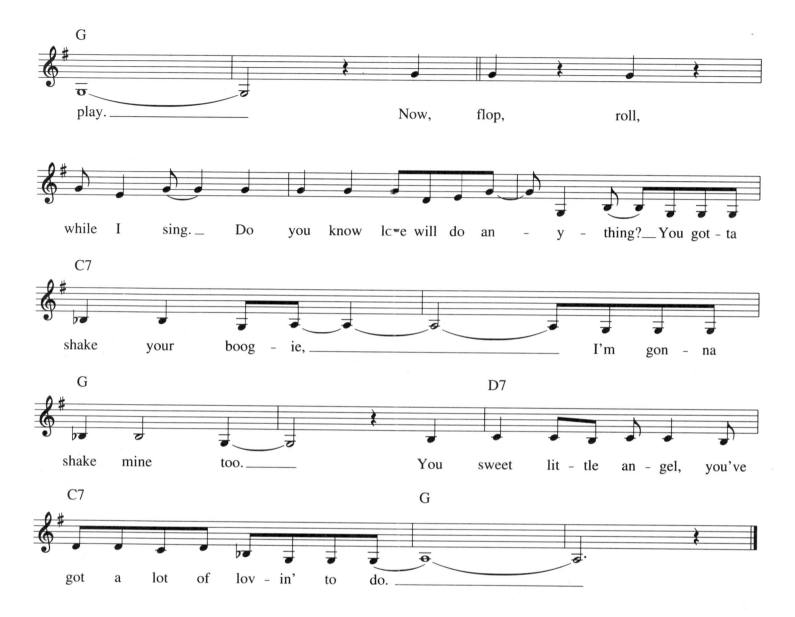

I'm Satisfied

Recorded by: Mississippi John Hurt

First in the country, then in the town, I'm a total shaker from my navel on down.
I'm satisfied, it's gonna bring you back.
I'm satisfied, tickled too, old enough to marry you.
I'm satisfied, it's gonna bring you back.

I pull my dress to my knees, I give my all to who I please.
I'm satisfied, it's gonna bring you back.
I'm satisfied, tickled too, old enough to marry you.
I'm satisfied, it's gonna bring you back.

Go Back to Your No Good Man

Recorded by: Lonnie Johnson

It's true you bake good jel - ly roll, _____ the

best I've ev - er found. _____ It's true you

bake good jel - ly roll, ____ it's the best I've ev - er found. __

_____ But, it's one thing you got - ta stop ma - ma, that's

serv - ing it all o - ver town. ___

Don't you think because I love you, you can play me for a chump to my face. (2x)
But I'm not as dumb as you think, there's another woman to fill your place.

Give me them clothes I bought you, take my diamonds off your hand. (2x)
Now, you just like I found you, go back to your handy man.

Now, I put shoes on your shoes on your feet when your bare feet was pattin' the ground. (2x)
While I was out slaving for you, you was chasin' every rat in town.

Now, woman I stuck with you when you didn't have a friend at all. (2x)
So give them shoes I bought you, and that wig, and let your head go bald.

Worry, Worry, Worry

Recorded by: B.B. King

Well, wor-ry, wor-ry, wor-ry, ___ wor-ry is all ___ I can

do. ___ Yes, wor-ry, wor-ry, wor-ry, ___

wor-ry is all I can do. ___ Yes, my

life is so mis-er-'ble, ba-by, ___ and it's all on ac-count of

you. ___

It hurt me so bad when you said that we were through. (2x)
I would rather be dead than be here, lonesome and blue.

Well, someday, baby, when the blood runs cold in my veins. (2x)
You won't be able to hurt me no more, 'cause my heart won't feel no pain.

You're Breaking My Heart

Recorded by B.B. King

Well, it's hard for me to believe, hard for me to believe you'd do me wrong.
Yes, please have mercy, baby, won't you stay here where you belong.
Well, I got the blues so bad, baby, sometimes you make me wish I was never born.

Yes, I thought I was your man, baby, I want to know why did you make me your fool.
Why did you let me love you so long, baby, why did you use me like a tool.
Well, you played a game with me, baby, you know you used the Devil's rule.